8
Steps
to High
Performance

MARC EFFRON

Steps to High Performance

Focus On
What You Can Change
(Ignore the Rest)

HARVARD BUSINESS REVIEW PRESS
BOSTON, MASSACHUSETTS

Copyright 2018 Harvard Business School Publishing Corporation
All rights reserved
Printed in the United States of America

10 9 8 7 6 5 4 3 2 1

The web addresses referenced in this book were live and correct at the time of the book's publication but may be subject to change.

Library of Congress cataloging-in-publication data is forthcoming

ISBN: 978-1-63369-397-5
eISBN: 978-1-63369-398-2

The paper used in this publication meets the requirements of the American National Standard for Permanence of Paper for Publications and Documents in Libraries and Archives Z39.48-1992.

So many people have shaped how I think about and approach my work on high performance. Thank you to everyone who has taught me, challenged me, supported me, and guided me over the years. My special thanks to my wife, Michelle, for her unfailing love and support for more than thirty years.

CONTENTS

FOREWORD

by Marshall Goldsmith

Marc Effron, author of *Leading the Way* and *One Page Talent Management,* offers an exceptional road map for achieving our highest potential and our greatest level of performance in this, his latest book, *8 Steps to High Performance.*

I immediately knew I was going to love this book when Marc told me he bases it on a statement made by the father of modern management, Peter Drucker. As with many of my own greatest insights on leadership, which are based on what I learned personally from Peter Drucker, Marc bases this work on Peter's philosophy: "Do not try to change yourself. You are unlikely to succeed. But work hard to improve the way you perform."

There are eight steps suggested in this exceptional book. All are important to your goal of achieving peak high performance. One on which I'd love to offer a little insight to you is step six, "Fake it." I love this step. Marc describes it as follows: "A high performer cares about showing the right behaviors, not being their 'genuine' self. You'll learn that faking behaviors works, why it's sometimes better than being the genuine you, and the situations where faking a new behavior matters most."

I refer to this as "Showtime." I am inspired by great theater. Every night, great performers pour their hearts into each production. Some have headaches, some have family problems, but it doesn't matter. When it's showtime, they give it all they have. Although it might be the thousandth time an actor has performed the part, it might be the first time the audience member sitting in the fourth row has seen the production. To the true performer, every night is opening night.

And like great actors, high achievers sometimes need to be consummate performers. When they need to motivate to get a project completed, to inspire people around them, or to build teams for certain projects that otherwise might not fit, they do it. It doesn't matter if they have a headache; it doesn't matter if they have a personality conflict. They do whatever it takes to help their organization succeed. When they need to be "on," like the Broadway stars, it's showtime. It's a tough lesson, but one that the greatest leaders I've ever met have learned and learned well.

This is just one of the many things you'll learn when you pick up *8 Steps to High Performance*. Because it is research-based and includes self-assessments and tools to gauge your progress in realizing the performance you are trying to achieve, it is an application book of the highest level.

Follow the eight steps that Marc outlines here and you will reach your peak performance goals!

Life is good.

—Marshall Goldsmith

The international best-selling author or editor of thirty-five books, including *What Got You Here Won't Get You There* and *Triggers*

PREFACE

I wish that, as a young man, someone had sat me down and said to me, "Marc, I'm going to tell you how to be highly successful at work. A few of the things I describe may come naturally to you, and others might require significant effort. You may believe that some of what I tell you will work well and that some won't. But I can promise that everything I tell you will help you to perform and, the more of it you do, the more successful you will be."

No one gave me that gift, and I doubt that many of you received it either. That's unfortunate, because the lack of those insights makes our quest for high performance more challenging than it needs to be. Since we don't know what has been proven to work, we do our best to sort through the performance advice we get from books, bosses, friends, and the internet. That advice may be highly accurate or total folklore; it's difficult to know which it is until we try it. Our quest for high performance is often guided by trial and error, as we do what we think is right and then hope for the best results.

It's even more unfortunate that these conversations don't occur because we know exactly what helps people to be high performers. That's correct. There is clear, conclusive science that describes exactly how individuals can improve their performance at work. These aren't platitudes like "keep your head down and work hard," but specific actions, such as how to set goals, how to behave in order to drive results, and how to accelerate your development. So, if these facts are well known, why don't those conversations happen?

The challenge is that those powerful, performance-improving insights are hidden in dusty academic journals like individual pieces of a larger puzzle. The average Jill or Joe isn't a PhD research scientist, so would never sort through the original research to find those insights or know how to assemble the many pieces into a coherent picture.

Perhaps most challenging, these insights are rarely presented in a way that you can practically apply them at work. When the insights occasionally find their way into a book or article, it's typically one written by a consultant or journalist who understands the topic but has never had to apply the concept in the real world. Their advice may be technically accurate, but it often ignores the practical realities of busy people, competing priorities, or unsupportive bosses.

If we could gather these great insights, sort through them to identify which matter most, and make them practical, applicable, and easy to understand, we could enable anyone to become a high performer. This knowledge would democratize high performance by making it available to everyone, rather than just a lucky, privileged few. That's the purpose of *8 Steps to High Performance*.

I wrote this book so that anyone can be a high performer. As a corporate executive and management consultant, I have seen too many smart people underperform because they didn't know or believe in the eight steps. These potential stars derailed their careers by relying on their one overwhelming strength for success (e.g., work harder; develop yourself even more) until they hit a performance wall by ignoring the other seven steps. Other leaders rejected great advice to build a network or change certain behaviors because they didn't believe it would improve their performance. All of these smart, highly capable people left performance on the table and lost out on the wonderful benefits that being a high performer brings.

Before we talk about high performance, let's define it. A high performer is someone who consistently delivers better results and behaviors, on an absolute and relative basis, than 75 percent of their peers. There are a few words in that sentence worth your extra attention. "Consistently" doesn't mean that you show an occasional flash of brilliance or sometimes deliver well on a project. It means that you regularly do those things. "Relative" means that your performance must be better than others', not just better than the goal. If you exceed your goal and all your peers far exceed the same goal, that's great. But, you're still underperforming compared to others.

The Journey to Eight

If there are eight steps to high performance, an obvious question is why there aren't seven or nine or twenty-five. Getting to eight was a journey that started with the publication of my last book (with coauthor Miriam Ort), *One Page Talent Management* (OPTM). We wrote OPTM to help corporate human resource leaders understand what was scientifically proven to be true about growing high-quality talent and the simplest way to implement those truths. Readers loved the science-based simplicity of the book, and we were gratified that many companies changed how they managed their talent because of that advice.

But I quickly recognized that much of that advice would never reach the ultimate customer, the employee. My goal wasn't that companies would build better corporate processes, but that more employees would become successful. I realized that if I connected directly with the customer about high performance, it would help to supplement the hard work that companies were doing in that area and help close the gap where they were falling short. You are my customer.

I spent the eight years between the publication of OPTM and writing *8 Steps* researching the science and practice of individual high performance. My goal was to apply the concept of "science-based simplicity" to identify which factors had the strongest scientific proof that they drove high performance and to determine the simplest, easiest way for someone to apply them. This meant that everything I included in *8 Steps* had to be conclusively proven to improve individual performance. This eliminated some novel concepts, but it ensured that everything I included in the book would be guaranteed to work.

To understand the science, I reviewed the extensive academic research on performance I had used in OPTM. For example, I knew that setting great goals and having better strategic fit with a company were scientifically proven to improve individual performance. It was clear that individual development would also have an impact on performance, even though there were far fewer insights available about exactly which capabilities someone should develop or how they could grow them.

At that point, the questions began to outnumber the answers. I knew that understanding and improving behaviors should be linked to higher performance, but were any specific behaviors guaranteed to deliver higher performance in every situation? What about networking? People spoke about it as being valuable, but was there any proof that it improved individual performance? What about areas like sleep, exercise, and nutrition?

The only way to determine what to include and what to leave out was to read the academic research on every possible performance topic and decide if the findings justified inclusion in the book. I read hundreds of articles and reviewed thousands of others on topics that did and didn't make the final list. The desired level of proof I sought in order to include a topic was a meta-analysis that concluded that these actions definitely improved individual performance at work.[1] That real-world validation was critical; studies using rats and undergraduates didn't count.

In addition to reading the academic literature, I pored through the most popular books and articles on how to improve individual performance. Most made claims that were quickly undercut by their lack of scientific proof. Others came closer to being scientific malpractice; people who should have known better saying fundamentally incorrect things. Few of the concepts from those popular business books, articles, and TED talks made the cut.

After reviewing thousands of articles on a multitude of topics, only eight topics met my standards to include in *8 Steps*. If you wonder why no one's ever summarized this information before, consider that effort. Briefly, the eight steps are:

- Step one—Set big goals: How to set goals that create higher performance

- Step two—Behave to perform: Which behaviors predict higher performance in different situations

- Step three—Grow yourself faster: How to most quickly grow the most important capabilities

- Step four—Connect: Who to connect with and why

- Step five—Maximize your fit: How to understand and adapt to your company's strategy

- Step six—Fake it: Why you sometimes shouldn't be the "genuine" you

- Step seven—Commit your body: How to best manage your body to sustain your performance

- Step eight—Avoid distractions: How to avoid management fads that distract you from high performance

I've personally seen each of these steps create successful leaders in every sector, industry, and part of the globe, in addition to being proven by the science. I've also seen very bright people fail when they ignore these fundamental truths.

As a staff assistant for a US congressman, I watched two very smart and capable leaders compete for the coveted chief of staff position. One leader focused on becoming a deep technical expert in how to craft and pass legislation. The other leader invested time to get to know other chiefs of staff, learn about the job, and build a strong network with those who might influence his future. When the congressman decided who to select as chief of staff, this leader's deep and extensive connections (step four, "connect") were the differentiating factor.

In consulting to large, complex companies worldwide, I have seen executives get left behind because they didn't understand that their company's new strategy demanded they work in a new way. In a large health-care organization, the CEO had grown the company from a startup to a thriving $5 billion company with more than five thousand employees. His entrepreneurial focus, disdain for process, and personal charisma had been critical for the company's success. Unfortunately, the larger company needed a leader who could build the infrastructure and operational discipline necessary to thrive at this size. This CEO refused to adapt his style to better fit with the company's changing needs (step five, "maximize your fit") and both lost his job and caused other executives to lose theirs.

I've seen leaders become high performers when they moved from setting fifteen to twenty goals to focusing on the few, most important things they could deliver to their company (step one, "set big goals"). Other leaders sought more-challenging career experiences and found that the larger, riskier moves accelerated their development (step three, "grow yourself faster").

Not New, Just Proven to Work

You may read some of the eight steps and say to yourself, "I've known that for years!" Exactly. The fact that the eight steps are well proven also means that they aren't new. They're the product of years of research by smart scientists around the world who've proven beyond a doubt that each step works. That should make you even more confident in the power of the eight steps. The challenge is that very few companies and individuals know all the steps or how to practically apply them for the best results.

The great news is that the eight steps are both proven to increase performance, and you can take all of them. Every chapter includes specific advice and practical tools that help you take each step. You can also be confident that the steps are valuable now and will be valuable for years because they're based on the strongest science about human behavior. While companies' preferences for how they manage people will change, the fundamental truths about human behavior and performance evolve over decades.

Who Will Benefit from *8 Steps to High Performance*

When I was writing *8 Steps to High Performance*, a senior colleague told me it would be a little embarrassing for him to carry around a book about how to be a high performer. After all, he said, at his age he should have "figured it all out." I guess that might be true if we had each been taught the eight steps when we were young and had regularly practiced them throughout our careers. Unfortunately, until now, no one has sorted through all of the science about human performance at work and translated the findings into simple, practical steps.

The quest for higher performance is worthwhile no matter what your career stage or circumstance. You may be starting your career and wondering how to best establish yourself in your company or profession. You might be an experienced professional who isn't advancing as fast or performing as strongly as you would like to. You may be a high performer but not understand which factors are responsible for your success and which might hurt your future performance. Unless you are the highest-performing individual in your industry or profession, there's at least one thing in this book that will help you to improve your performance.

While I hope you'll personally benefit from this book, I'm confident that your team members will benefit from having a copy. It's likely that much of the advice I offer aligns with how you already coach your employees, so you can use *8 Steps* to reinforce your messages. The simple assessments and tools in the book will allow them to have even greater accountability to increase their performance.

Many people approach me at industry conferences with a dog-eared, flagged copy of my last book and explain that they use it as a reference guide whenever they have questions about how to manage talent. I hope that you will use *8 Steps* in the same way. Ideally, it will be an always-ready reference that can provide guidance, a tool, or a tip whenever you need it.

About Your Real and Perceived Boundaries

The subtitle of *8 Steps* is "Focus on what you can change (ignore the rest)." You'll notice that attitude reflected throughout the book. I'll describe exactly what can help you be a high performer and how to apply that idea at work. I'll ask you to set aside any excuses and explanations for why you can't be a high performer. That doesn't mean that I don't understand the boundaries and limitations we each have or empathize with those who have difficult work or personal situations.

You may have a challenging home life, care for an aging parent, be a single mother, or already feel overwhelmed by the number of things that fight for your attention each day. At work, you might have a difficult boss, a job that doesn't engage you, or nasty coworkers, or work in a failing company. I understand these difficult challenges and ask, given that situation, how can you use your remaining time, focus, and energy to be a higher performer? Pick the one step that you can take today. After you make great progress on that step, move to the next one. Your journey to high performance might move more slowly than others, but at least you will be confident that you're on the right path.

Take the Challenge

The path to complete the eight steps is straightforward, but it's not easy. It requires that you desire to be a high performer, work hard to achieve each step, and avoid the distractions that will tempt you along the way. The benefits you'll receive from being a high performer make the work and sacrifice a smart investment.

You'll increase your earning power. You'll learn more and move up faster. You'll get exposure and opportunities that are unavailable to others. The only thing you need to do is to commit yourself to success, believe in your abilities, and take the eight steps to high performance.

8
Steps
to High
Performance

How to Be a High Performer

Some people begin their careers with a clear performance advantage. They may be smarter than you, come from a better socio-economic background, be physically attractive, or have helpful personality characteristics. Each of those factors is scientifically proven to help someone perform better than you. Those combined items predict up to 50 percent of anyone's individual performance, according to academic research.[1] Let's call those things the "fixed 50 percent" because they're largely unchangeable once we become adults.

Of course, there's no guarantee that someone with more fixed 50 percent qualities will be a high performer, but it means that some people begin with a clear head start. A great-looking, highly intelligent, naturally hard-working, not-too-offensive person from a middle- or upper-class background enters their career more likely than you to be a high performer. They may still fail miserably, but it won't be because they didn't start with a healthy advantage.

That's not fair, and it may make you believe that high performance at work is largely out of your control. But, fortunately, that's just the fixed 50 percent. You control every other factor that drives your performance, from your capabilities and behaviors to the size of your network to your personal development. We know about those factors thanks to thousands of researchers who have studied every possible performance driver, from goal setting to how we learn to the quality of our sleep. Let's call these combined areas the "flexible 50 percent"; you have the power to shape them at will.

The challenge for someone who wants to be a high performer is to sort through that overwhelmingly large amount of information, identify what really matters, and practically put it to use. *8 Steps* simplifies and focuses that voluminous research into what's scientifically proven to increase performance and how to apply it to be a high performer.

Why Be a High Performer?

A good place to start our discussion is to answer the question, "What's the benefit of being a high performer?" High performance will get you more of what you value, whether that's flexibility, power, opportunity, pay, or recognition. It creates the foundation for a successful career. It gives you access to parts of your company that you wouldn't otherwise see. These benefits happen because organizations love high performers. They understand that high performers create and sustain successful companies. They'll work hard to identify their best performers and give those outstanding employees more time, attention, development, and compensation to make sure that they're engaged and that they don't leave.

The company's additional investment is a smart choice because the science says that high-performing employees deliver anywhere between 100 percent and 500 percent more output than their average- or below-average-performing coworkers.[2] They contribute more, so they get more. That doesn't mean that average performers are worth less, but they are unlikely to receive the same investment as top performers.

As an employee, you should also care about being a high performer because it gets you closer to your next promotion. While there's no guarantee that you'll get the next big opportunity only because of your strong performance, you will be much better positioned than others.

If you think your organization is different, that it values everyone equally or that high performance isn't its primary concern, consider a recent study on corporate culture published in *Harvard Business Review*. In this study, more than 250 companies were asked to select their dominant culture style from among eight categories. Their choices included cultures dominated by caring, purpose, enjoyment, and others. In 89 percent of those companies, they defined their dominant culture style as "results."[3] Results means performance. Culture styles like purpose or learning were selected by only 9 percent and 7 percent of respondents, respectively. This reinforces that almost every organization's primary concern is high performance.

I also know how much companies value high performance because I advise the world's largest and most complex companies on this topic. Our consulting firm creates strategies to identify high performers, develop them, and keep them highly engaged. Companies understand the massive benefits that high performers produce, and they want more of them, now. They want to invest in selecting and growing their best talent and to upgrade (that typically means fire) those who will never be high performers.

What's Really True about High Performance?

When you try to understand what's proven to increase performance, it's easy to be distracted by the daily barrage of nonscientific stories on the topic ("Relax Like a Pro: 5 Steps to Hacking Your Sleep") and the clickbait links that ask if actions like starving ourselves will make us more focused at work.[4] (Note: the Yale University researchers' answer to that question was yes.) Those stories typically have little to do with real science, or they highlight a juicy finding or two out of context. Either way, they don't give you any practical guidance about how to apply those nuggets of information.

It pays to be cautious even when someone claims that something is "scientifically proven." In the *New York Times* best-seller *Outliers*, Malcolm Gladwell wrote a chapter based on scientific research that said anyone could master a skill with ten thousand hours of practice.[5] The media broadly retold that story, and it's been cited more than six thousand times in scholarly books and articles. Unfortunately, it's not true, and other scientists quickly proved that less than one-third of someone's performance is due to their hours of practice.[6]

If you want to be a high performer, you need to be a cautious consumer of these claims. To assess whether a statement about high performance is believable, sort that statement into one of three categories—is it research, science, or conclusive science? You'll need to decide which level of proof you require to believe a claim.

- *Research:* A consulting firm conducts a study and reports the results, often to support a product or service that it sells. Its findings may be true, but there's no independent verification. The consulting firm typically won't allow anyone to verify if its claims are true.

- *Science:* Someone conducts a carefully designed experiment to test a hypothesis (i.e., if we select job candidates based on their intelligence, we will get higher-performing employees). They publish their research process and findings in a peer-reviewed academic journal. Others can read about that experiment and draw their own conclusions about the findings.

- *Conclusive science:* Other scientists conduct the same experiment described tens or hundreds of times. Almost every time, the conclusions are the same. This is a very strong suggestion that the findings are conclusively true and is the strongest level of proof.

Each of the eight steps is based on conclusive science; I use the terms "science" or "research" in the book when referring to concepts or examples at those lower standards of proof. I've included hundreds of citations so you can review the actual research, science, or conclusive science that prove the eight steps.

The Eight Steps

What do you control that's scientifically proven to improve your performance? The conclusive science suggests eight steps that will help you be a high performer:

- Step one—Set big goals: Goals have incredible power to focus and motivate us; more focus and motivation positions you for high performance. I'll explain how to identify the few goals that matter and stretch your expectations for what you can deliver. You'll learn the ideal type of coaching that will help you hit your elevated performance expectations.

- Step two—Behave to perform: All behaviors are not created equal. You'll learn which behaviors you're most likely to display, how to avoid going off the rails, and how to change your behaviors to the ones that drive high performance. You'll also learn how to identify the behaviors that your company values most.

- Step three—Grow yourself faster: You're more likely to be a high performer if you're more capable in the areas your company cares about most. You'll learn the optimal balance of experiences, education, and feedback that will accelerate your development. You'll create your own personal experience map to accelerate and guide your development.

- Step four—Connect: The old saying isn't completely true, but who you know does matter, and the strength of your relationship with them matters even more. You'll learn how to build a powerful network inside and outside of work, even if your introverted nature makes that your number one fear.

- Step five—Maximize your fit: People deliver best when they "fit" their work environment; that means a misfit can turn a potential high performer into an average one. You'll learn how to identify the scenarios in which you fit best and how to change your fit to improve your performance.

- Step six—Fake it: You may have heard or read about being a "genuine" or "authentic" leader. We'll explain why being the "fake" you is sometimes a better choice for higher performance and how to adjust your behaviors to what's ideal for success at different points in your career.

- Step seven—Commit your body: Your body plays a powerful role in your ability to deliver, and it's the only performance lever that you completely control. You'll learn how sleep supports great performance and the surprising performance effects of exercise and diet.

- Step eight—Avoid distractions: Understanding which advice—no matter how popular and how many books it's sold—is simply not helpful can be a challenge. To that end, step eight is to know and avoid the performance fads that suggest easy answers to difficult performance questions that distract you from the proven steps.

I've been asked which topic I thought would make the book's final list but didn't. The answer is exercise. Before reading the voluminous research on exercise, I would have sworn that there was a strong relationship between being in great shape and being a higher performer. While being in poor shape will indirectly lower your performance through increased health issues, it turns out that more trips to the gym each week won't meaningfully benefit anything other than your waistline.

The eight steps are straightforward but not easy. They require that you have the interest, commitment, and passion to be a high performer at work. If that's your vision, I'll help you achieve each step. A good starting point is to understand which steps you've already mastered and which you should practice to achieve. The eight-step quick audit will give you some insight (see table I-1).

TABLE I-1

Eight-step quick audit: Where are you today?

Instructions: Let's keep this simple: "Yes" means that you conclusively do this; "No" means that you don't.

	The eight steps
Yes/No	**Performance mindset:** I acknowledge that high performance at work requires additional time, effort, and personal sacrifice.
Yes/No	**Step one—Set big goals:** I have a few big, challenging goals at work and seek regular coaching to improve my performance.
Yes/No	**Step two—Behave to perform:** I understand how my personality and "derailers" affect my performance. I regularly seek insights to improve my behaviors.
Yes/No	**Step three—Grow yourself faster:** I have identified the specific experiences that will most accelerate my career growth and am in or actively pursuing the next key experience.
Yes/No	**Step four—Connect:** I regularly improve the strength of my key connections inside and outside my organization.
Yes/No	**Step five—Maximize your fit:** I know which capabilities and behaviors my company will value most in the next two to four years and am changing myself to better align with those needs.
Yes/No	**Step six—Fake it:** I adjust my behaviors as needed to optimize my performance rather than always trying to be the genuine me.
Yes/No	**Step seven—Commit your body:** I optimize my sleep and exercise schedules to support high performance and use science-proven strategies to compensate when I don't.
Yes/No	**Step eight—Avoid distractions:** I am a careful consumer of performance advice and only do what's scientifically proven to make me a high performer at work.

Where you answered no, list the top three steps in which you'd like to make progress. You can start reading any step, so consider reading these steps first.

Priority area 1 is Step #_____

Priority area 2 is Step #_____

Priority area 3 is Step #_____

What You Should Know about the Fixed 50 Percent

While the eight steps will make you a high performer, it's helpful to understand how fixed 50 percent factors like personality influence your behaviors and performance. Then you will understand which of the eight steps come naturally to you and which will require more effort. While the fixed 50 percent gives some people the *potential* for higher performance, it doesn't guarantee it.

For example, if you're in a one-hundred-meter race and three other runners start two, five, and ten meters ahead of you, each has a starting advantage. After the starter's pistol fires, preparation, motivation, and skill decide who moves how far, how fast. If you've trained harder, eaten smarter, and understand the mechanics of sprinting better than they do, you can make up their initial advantage and win the race.

Your intelligence, core personality, body, and socioeconomic background are the uncontrollable fixed 50 percent factors.

Your Intelligence

Blame your mom and dad for this one, but how smart you are (as measured by IQ) is about 50 percent inherited and predicts up to 25 percent of your performance.[7] Intelligence is the single largest predictor of performance, and it's twice as powerful as any other element. The good news is that if your IQ is in the high average range (110–119 on an IQ test), you're likely smart enough to be a high performer in many situations. The average college graduate's IQ is 115.[8] Higher IQ does matter more if your job is more complex (i.e., rocket scientist), but an IQ that's too high can make you a less effective manager.[9]

Intelligence is in the fixed 50 percent because it's largely hard-wired by the time we're in our late teens. We can still learn after that, of course, but our fundamental level of intelligence doesn't change in a meaningful way. If you believe that you know more now than you did when you were eighteen, that's true but irrelevant. Consider a computer's processing chip versus its memory chip. Its processing chip sorts through data so it can complete an activity and the chip can operate up to, but not higher than, its preset speed. That processing chip is like your intelligence—there is a maximum speed with which you can process information. Your computer's memory chip can store large amounts of information, and you can add more chips (more knowledge) to store even more information. Those memory chips are your knowledge. You can add more chips over time, but the speed with which you can process information (your intelligence) doesn't meaningfully change.

Your Core Personality

Another gift from your parents is your core personality, which, like intelligence, is about 50 percent inherited. Your core personality is shaped by what you've experienced through your early twenties, and it can change slightly over time, but it's largely set as you enter the working world.[10]

I use the term "core" personality because, while your core personality guides your behaviors, you still completely control your behaviors. For example, if you're naturally more extroverted, you might have been told early in your career that you speak a lot in team meetings and need to give others a chance to participate. You corrected that behavior, but it didn't change your core personality—you learned how to behave differently. Your core personality trait of being extroverted means you're naturally oriented to behave a certain way, not that you're unable to behave differently. That *choice* of how you behave makes a critical difference between your core personality and how people experience you at work.

Your Body

Falling squarely into the "not fair" category is the fact that your body influences your ability to succeed. People who are tall as adolescents or adults have higher social esteem and performance, and earn an extra 1 percent to 2 percent of income for each additional inch they are above average.[11] Given this persistent and well-known relationship, some scientists have even suggested taxing tall people to balance out their unfair "unearned income"![12]

Beauty matters, too, with more attractive people both earning more and being seen as more intelligent, even though there's little relationship between looks and smarts.[13] Weight bias reduces the likelihood that heavier people will be hired and receive high performance ratings.[14] Gender doesn't affect performance ratings; women typically receive slightly higher ratings than men but lower pay increases.[15] Race bias occurs globally and, despite positive words and plentiful investments, is pervasive and not disappearing quickly enough.

Again, that's all unfair, but keep in mind that Mahatma Gandhi was five foot four, and rock star Bono is five foot seven. There's a relationship between height and income, but height doesn't perfectly predict your income. More women and minorities are (slowly) filling CEO positions. As for beauty, executive suites are full of high-performing people who will never grace the cover of *Vogue* or *GQ*. Continue to fight against all those other unfair biases, but work hard to master the controllable, flexible 50 percent.

Your Socioeconomic Background

Your socioeconomic background is one of the greatest predictors of your academic achievement; it predicts both future capabilities and the colleges and universities you're most likely to attend.[16] If you attend a highly ranked school, you'll likely have higher-quality professors, more-intelligent classmates, and a greater range of job opportunities after graduation then someone who attends a lower-ranked school. That's unfair, uncontrollable, and not worth worrying about after graduation day.

The fixed 50 percent factors are powerful and largely unchangeable, but they're responsible for, at most, 50 percent of how you perform. There are probably hundreds of other obstacles to high performance at work—a bad boss, a challenging economy, unsupportive coworkers, bad luck—but the path to high performance remains. Looking at the flexible 50 percent versus the fixed 50 percent, it's clear that you control an amazing amount of your own performance (see figure I-1). If you execute the eight steps well, you can be an incredibly high performer at work and overcome any initial, fixed 50 percent disadvantages.

FIGURE I-1

The flexible 50 percent versus the fixed 50 percent

The flexible 50 percent (changeable)
- How you set goals
- How you behave
- How you develop
- How you network
- How you present yourself
- How you manage your sleep

The fixed 50 percent (unchangeable)
- Your intelligence
- Your core personality
- Your socioeconomic background
- Your race/gender/basic physical appearance

On Becoming a High Performer

Some other things to consider on your journey to high performance include sacrifice and balance, high potential, relative performance, depending on yourself, and getting out of your own way.

Sacrifice and Balance

You can only achieve high performance when you have a high performer's mindset. That mindset is one of competitive edge and self-sacrifice, and prioritizing performance at work above your other options. The ongoing debate about the intersection of work and nonwork activities questions the possibility of "having it all." The premise that it's possible to have it all is challenged by any typical definition of "all." The pursuit of high performance means that you try to maximize your success at work. That makes it very difficult to also maximize any other time-consuming activity. You can slice your time pie any way you want, but a larger slice in one area requires a smaller slice somewhere else.

High performers typically work more hours than average performers. Simple logic explains why. If two equally skilled and motivated people engage in an activity and one person spends 25 percent more time on it, that person will produce more results, on average. The additional time they invest at work creates a virtuous cycle. More work means more learning has occurred, so that person becomes more capable and potentially a better contributor in the future. Her higher performance from her additional hours becomes known in the organization, so she receives additional opportunities to show her skills. She might get more exposure to senior leaders who can serve as sponsors or mentors. Her success isn't guaranteed because she's put in more hours, but she will be more likely to succeed than those who work fewer hours.

Occasionally I hear the cry, "I'm really efficient at work. I get as much done in forty hours as others do in fifty hours." That may be true, but it still comes at a cost. When people say they're more efficient, they often mention how they avoid social activities like chatting with others in the breakroom or how they frequently work from home to avoid the distractions of the office. While these behaviors may make someone more efficient in the total hours they spend at work, they're not building the important relationships they will need to succeed and advance in every organization.

In addition, if you accomplish the same amount of work in less time than your coworker, you're not a high performer—you're efficient. You haven't delivered anything more than an average performer. You're just a very fast, average performer. More hours invested means more time that you can spend on all the steps to high performance. Being efficient is great, but you still must do more and better than others to be a high performer.

High performance at work requires that you prioritize work performance over other activities. You can be flexible in how and where you apply these additional hours, but more hours, up to a point, are an essential ingredient in high performance.

High Performance Is Not High Potential

Many people confuse high performance (doing your job exceptionally well today) with high potential (being able to do bigger, more complex jobs tomorrow). While being a high performer is a necessary threshold for being considered high potential, it's just the first step. High performance today only predicts high performance tomorrow in similar situations. If you're a great coder today, you'll likely be a great coder tomorrow and maybe can learn other coding languages. Your strength in coding doesn't predict that you can manage other coders or lead an IT architecture team or excel in any other technical role.

Performance Is Relative

It's not just your own performance that makes you a high performer, but how your performance compares to others'. Let's assume that you and Susie have similar sales territories and identical products to sell. You hit 125 percent of your goal. Great job! Susie hits 150 percent of her goal. You had a great year, but Susie had a better year—she's a higher performer. That doesn't mean you should treat coworkers like competitors, but you should recognize the real standard of performance is measured by how it compares to the best results. You'll be evaluated not just for what you deliver but also relative to how others perform. That's going to be true throughout your life, and it's best to recognize and embrace that. You don't have to be the best at everything. Just remember that someone else is trying to be the best at anything that you do.

Depending On Yourself

You may believe that your company will (or should) give you the support, guidance, and tools to become a high performer. Some companies might and others might not, but it's a risky strategy to outsource your performance and success to your employer. The first step to take before any of the eight steps in this book is to acknowledge that you're accountable for your high performance.

Getting Out of Your Own Way

Do you know the comment, "He is his own worst enemy"? It's a wonderful summary of how our brains sometimes work against us being high performers. Your brain's core function is to ensure that you survive and, beyond its pursuit of food, shelter, and a mate, it works hard to preserve your self-image and self-esteem.[17] Its attempt to preserve your self-image creates some very challenging barriers to improving your performance, including:

- We externalize failure: We're prone to give ourselves credit for our successes and blame others for our failures. If you had a great sales year, it's because you put in significant effort and worked hard on your interpersonal skills. If you didn't meet your sales goals, it's because the territory you were given was too large, too small, too poor, or too competitive. This self-serving bias makes it difficult to honestly assess our performance and behaviors.[18]

- We mistakenly assign intent to others' actions: "Mary did that to make me look bad in the meeting!" is an example of how we assign a purpose to others' actions, even though this may not have been the person's intent. Mary likely said something in the meeting to prove a point she believed in and didn't consider you when she said it. When we come to those false conclusions, it's called fundamental attribution error; it can damage relationships and erode the interpersonal trust that supports our performance.[19]

- We ignore information that can help us perform: If we were perfectly rational human beings and wanted to improve our performance, we would carefully consider every piece of information we received about our performance.

Strangely, our brain works against us because it seeks out information that reinforces our self-image and ignores information that doesn't. We're surrounded by information that can help us perform better, but we often miss the opportunity to listen for it and apply it. That's called confirmation bias; it can give us a very inaccurate view of how we behave and perform and how others perceive us.[20]

While these biases can trip up your performance, once you recognize them, you can radically reduce their influence. We'll highlight how to do this in step two, "behave to perform."

Achieve Your Theoretical Maximum Performance

Scientists who study the biomechanics of the human body give us a great benchmark for high performance at work—theoretical maximum performance. That is the theoretical maximum amount of weight someone can lift if their form, nutrition, adrenaline level, and so on is in perfect harmony. It's impossible to ever lift that amount of weight, but the concept of theoretical maximum can help us to understand that your maximum performance is far higher than what you deliver today.

For example, when the average Joe goes to the gym and lifts weights, the most weight he can lift is about 65 percent of his theoretical maximum. Highly trained athletes typically lift about 80 percent of their theoretical maximum. In Olympic competition, weight lifters often reach 92 percent or 93 percent of their theoretical maximum. That Olympian can lift about 50 percent more than the average person but, more importantly, almost 15 percent more than already highly accomplished athletes.[21]

Think about your performance at work in the exact same way. How close can you get to your theoretical maximum performance if you perfectly apply what we know about human performance? *8 Steps* is all about helping you go from strong effort to your theoretical maximum performance. When you finish this book, you'll understand which factors will help move you toward your theoretical maximum and how to best apply them. Like weight lifters, you'll learn that success isn't just about pushing harder to lift more weight but about optimizing every element of your drive, mindset, and capabilities to win.

Let's Get Started

You now know about the flexible 50 percent that you can control, the fixed 50 percent that you can't, and the new standard of theoretical maximum performance. *8 Steps* gives you the practical, science-based guidance and tools to reach new heights of performance as fast as possible. The advice you read will be very transparent: what works, what doesn't, and how to apply science to be a high performer. It's better to be shocked into reality now than waste years on the wrong tactics or in the wrong company. Not every boss or company will be honest with you about what it takes to be a high performer at work—I will.

Let's get started.

Set Big Goals

D eliver big results. It's the heart of high performance and the critical step before you worry about any of the next seven steps. The great news about delivering big results is that powerful science tells us exactly how to do it well; the fundamentals haven't changed in ages.

Consider Michelangelo. In 1506, Pope Julius II decided to commission the painting of the Sistine Chapel ceiling and asked the artist Michelangelo to accept the challenge. Michelangelo should have considered this to be the commission of a lifetime, but he wasn't interested. He was primarily a sculptor, not a painter, and the prospect of working suspended from the ceiling through a Roman summer didn't appeal to him. At the time, he was also busy sculpting the future tomb of that same Pope Julius, so he could honestly tell Julius, "I'm overloaded now but thanks for thinking of me." Michelangelo's challenge was that Julius paid for much of his work and Michelangelo was also a devout Catholic, so eventually he felt compelled to take the job.

Julius thought the ceiling should feature large paintings of the twelve apostles, a vision he communicated to Michelangelo. Michelangelo offered a much grander option that included hundreds of figures and powerful images that would illustrate major Old and New Testament stories. He convinced Julius that this bolder, riskier vision would deliver on the original goal but with far superior results. He soon began to paint (standing up, not, as legend would have it, lying on his back).

Although Michelangelo's biblical knowledge was so extensive that it could easily guide his painting, he also brought in a famous theologian, Augustinian friar Giles of Viterbo, as an expert consultant. The result was, as we now know, impressive not just to Michelangelo and Julius but to the hundreds of millions of people who have viewed the Sistine Chapel ceiling since it was completed in 1511.

More than five hundred years after Michelangelo's Sistine Chapel experience with his boss Julius II, the formula to deliver big results through goals and coaching remains the same. Michelangelo's goals were:

- Aligned: Julius gave Michelangelo an initial goal for the Sistine Chapel ceiling design. Michelangelo agreed with the basic goal but suggested another way to accomplish it, given his unique knowledge and expertise. There was top-down direction and bottom-up fine-tuning.

- Promised: Michelangelo told Julius that he had too many other priorities at that time. Julius didn't add to the list but instead reprioritized the ceiling as Michelangelo's primary goal. Julius recognized that great performance required Michelangelo to focus on the vital few things and fully commit to them.

- Increased: Even with Michelangelo's formidable painting skills, creating a masterpiece on the Sistine Chapel's ceiling was a massive and risky endeavor. There was huge potential for failure and embarrassment. While Julius set a clear goal, Michelangelo's vision massively stretched the goal for "paint the chapel ceiling."

- Framed: Julius and Michelangelo agreed to a specific, important and measurable goal: paint a masterpiece on the ceiling of the Sistine Chapel. This created focus on the only thing that mattered—delivery of a masterpiece—and appropriately ignored all of the subtasks that would be required to achieve it.

Michelangelo also recognized that a great coach could help guide him to superior results. He was deeply familiar with the Bible and could have executed his vision of the chapel ceiling through his own thorough knowledge of biblical characters and stories. Instead, he took coaching and guidance from others who knew the subject well.

Why It Matters

Michelangelo could have painted a very attractive ceiling that met Julius's goals but that would never be considered great art. He could have complained about his full schedule and the unpleasant conditions, or that painting wasn't his "real" job. He could have painted his personal vision rather than finding an expert to guide him. Whether he knew it or not, by going against his natural instincts, Michelangelo became a case study on how to deliver better results by setting great goals.

Bigger goals, focused on the right things, allow you to demonstrate higher performance. Bigger goals also test your capabilities and build self-confidence in your ability to deliver great results in the future. Since bigger goals are also more challenging to achieve, you're forced to build new skills and capabilities to achieve them. In doing that, you grow faster than people with less challenging goals. Step one to high performance is to set big goals.

What We Know

Scientists have studied for years why humans perform and have given us amazing insights that can directly improve our performance. At the heart of that science is motivation—the push that makes you deliver. We're motivated to deliver either because we enjoy what we're doing (intrinsic motivation) and/or because we'll get something we value when we complete it (extrinsic motivation). Goals can create motivation and help you to apply it in a productive way.[1] There's a fixed 50 percent component to goals since people with certain personality characteristics are more motivated to perform, but you control your planning, effort, and execution.[2]

The conclusive science on goal setting says:

- Goals matter. It's a fundamental scientific fact—goals improve performance. When you have specific goals, you perform better than if you just try hard to achieve something. Consider a situation in which your manager tells you and an equally capable coworker to sell widgets. She tells your coworker to sell as many widgets as he can. She gives you a specific (high) sales goal. The science says that your specific goal will create the focus and motivation that will produce bigger results than someone who simply tries their hardest. People with goals almost always outdeliver people without goals at the same task.[3]

- Bigger goals increase what you deliver. Bigger goals motivate us to deliver bigger results since we're hardwired as humans to respond to a challenge by giving more effort. If I challenge you to jump one foot in the air, you'll try to do it. If I say jump two feet in the air, you'll try, even if you think you can't, and the more motivated you are, the closer you'll get to your theoretical maximum performance. You'll only stop trying to jump higher when either the reward for jumping no longer motivates you or you're too physically exhausted to try. The theoretical maximum performance principle suggests that you can perform 20 percent to 40 percent above what you typically deliver.[4]

- **Fewer goals mean higher achievement.** A deceptively powerful finding is that having a few goals is better for strong performance than having many. The power of goals comes from their ability to focus and motivate you, and having too many goals removes that focus. Science says that we put less effort into each additional goal we pursue, which means that having many goals isn't ambitious, it's counterproductive.[5] Doing three things extremely well is better than struggling to achieve six, eight, or twelve.

- **Coach toward the future.** Coaching combines feedback with direction—here's what you're doing today and here's how to do it better tomorrow. Strong science says that feedback increases performance and the best results come when that feedback is about activities, not behaviors. People also respond better to feedback that doesn't conflict with their self-image, so forward-looking guidance ("you might want to consider doing . . .") rather than backward-looking evaluation ("you did a poor job") is more likely to create change that increases performance.[6] There's much more about how to get (and give) great coaching in the step two, "behave to perform."

What to Do

Setting bigger goals ensures that what you plan to deliver is important enough for others to care about. Your focus on fewer, bigger goals doesn't mean that you should ignore important tasks or work less overall. It means that you understand which tasks add the most value to your organization. The "fewer, bigger" mindset also separates high performers from those who just want to perform the minimum requirements of their job. High performers want to meaningfully overachieve in the areas that matter most to the company—they promise big and deliver big. When you try to over-achieve, there's a larger risk for failure as well, but you will never be a high performer unless you take the risk to outperform.

Many of you write goals as part of your company's performance management process. You use your company's approach, your manager plays a role in helping set goals, and you may have to use a specific technology solution, and so on. My advice is written with that in mind. If you're not in a corporate environment and don't have those constraints, all the advice still applies, and you can avoid the corporate bureaucracy that can makes goal setting unpleasant.

There is a simple process to set goals that drive high performance—align, promise, increase, frame (see figure 1-1).

Align

You can only be a high performer if you work on what your company values most, so you need to understand which company or depart-ment objectives are more important than others. In some organi-zations, goals are translated from the top of the company or your department to each level below. In that case, getting direction may

FIGURE 1-1

How to set great goals

Align		Promise		Increase		Frame
Ensure upward alignment	▶	Few (3), prioritized	▶	Maximum stretch for all	▶	SIMple

be as simple as being told, "Here's what you need to work on." If your instructions aren't that clear, try this to get the right alignment:

- **Ask.** Ask your manager, "Based on the department's and the company's priorities, where do you want me to focus my efforts next year (or quarter)?" or "What are the three most important things you'd like me to accomplish next year?" You can also play to their self-interest and ask, "Which one of your goals can I best help you deliver and how?"

- **Research.** Review your company, department, or function strategy. Given your role, identify three big things you can deliver that will most help to achieve the strategy. If strategy documents aren't easily available, look at your company's investor relations or "about" website pages. There's almost always an executive presentation that describes the current year's priorities. You can also interpret what you've heard from your group, department, or company leader.

You should review your answers from the second option with your manager to ensure that you have accurately translated your company's strategy into your individual goals.

Promise

A new mindset is the essential starting point for setting bigger goals. Eliminate from your mind any past beliefs about how to choose a goal. Ask yourself, "What are the three big promises I will make to my organization this year?" This new framing shifts your thinking from things you need to do to what you'll deliver. You're not just highlighting a few job responsibilities and calling them goals. You're personally committing to deliver bigger results in the areas that matter most to your manager, department, and company.

Using the word "promise" rather than "goal" may sound like nothing more than a cute word trick. But that change in language elevates the seriousness and emotional commitment of what you've stated. There's a difference between saying you have a goal to complete a project by September and promising that you'll complete the project by September.

THREE BIG PROMISES. In many companies, people set far more goals than the number of truly important things they need to accomplish. This is sometimes driven by their manager, a need to be recognized for doing the "little stuff," or their belief that goal setting is a form of project management. The science says that focus matters; it's an area where many people undercut their performance by adding needless complexity. Their long list of goals obscures which goals are most important and makes it a challenge to understand where to focus their effort.

Consider these three goals:

- Launch new customer relationship management system with 90 percent user satisfaction.

- Open the Gurgaon, India, office and staff it with high-performing talent.

- Decrease production defects by 10 percent.

Those may sound like goals you would typically include in your long list of objectives. But in a "fewer, bigger" environment, those three promises would be the only three goals you're allowed. You would have identified them as the most important things you could possibly deliver this year or quarter. You would have dozens of other things to accomplish during the year, but you would state that delivering these three promises would make a larger contribution than anything else you could do. You could certainly add another goal, but you would first have to remove one of these.

Also, those brief statements are the goals in their entirety. There are no bullets underneath describing the fifteen tasks you plan to execute to achieve the goal. Your objective is to deliver on the promise you made, not to get credit for doing activities that contribute to that goal. Either you meet the goal or you don't.

Most leaders underperform at goal setting because they have too many, too small goals that are not prioritized. Two surefire tactics to choose fewer goals are (1) to combine activities into the larger promises, and (2) to prioritize promises.

COMBINE ACTIVITIES INTO PROMISES. If you've chosen a typical set of goals, at least some sound like activities. You may have included items on your goal list like "Hire new Ruby on Rails programmer" or "Contract with new supplier for gluten flour." Both are important activities, but are they really the big promises you're making to the company to improve its performance?

The actual big promise for that first statement may be "Launch new XYZ app by third quarter." A Ruby on Rails programmer would be an important step to achieve that, but it's not a meaningful enough deliverable to include as a goal. The promise for the second statement might be "Launch new gluten-free bread by June 1." Gluten-free flour is an essential ingredient for that type of bread, but finding a new supplier only contributes to your ability to launch. You shouldn't get rewarded for taking one step toward the goal, even if it saves money or time.

The good news is that the activities people typically list as goals are good raw material for those larger promises. Your opportunity is to combine that raw material into something that will make a meaningful difference to your company.

PRIORITIZE PROMISES. Even if you (or your boss) consider all your goals to be critical, a few always matter more than others. Identifying the priority promises starts with reviewing your company's or department's business objectives. Read those objectives and then consider your list of promises. Which of your promises has the most potential to meaningfully advance the progress against one of those objectives? One easy way to find the answer is to stack rank all your goals (create a list in order of impact) from the most to the least important. Stack ranking is a helpful exercise in any situation where you need to choose among many valuable things. Simply list the goals in order of importance, using any criteria you like—business impact, department priorities, your manager's requests, and so on. Once you complete the stack ranking, your priority promises should become clear.

Increase

To get closer to your theoretical maximum performance, you'll need to increase what you promise. Remember that science has clearly found that bigger goals deliver bigger results, so increasing the challenge of your goals should help your performance. Bigger goals will also help you grow, since you'll need to learn new ways to accomplish tasks to meet the larger goals you've set.

Bigger doesn't mean unrealistic or unachievable, but that you find a way to improve on your promise in one of these ways:

- Speed. You'll get the project done earlier, the process to run faster, or the sales cycle to be shorter than it has been.

- Quality. You'll reduce the number of defects, increase the number of satisfied customers, or improve the look or feel of the product by an amount that puts you among the world's best at that activity.

- Cost. You'll sell a product or service for more, or you'll reduce the cost of delivering it.

- Quantity. You'll sell, produce, or ship more of a product or service.

The pivotal question is, how much will you improve one of these elements? Start by asking yourself what it would take to be 20 percent better at any of the items listed. If that's an unreasonable stretch, try 15 percent. The difference must be enough so that your high performance will be meaningfully better than others and noticed by those who care about your results. One great measure of a bigger goal: you should be a little scared about your ability to achieve it.

Frame

Now that you have a few, big, aligned promises, you need to write them in a way that succinctly tells your manager what you're promising to achieve. That may sound easy, but most of us fail in this step by being too lengthy, complex, and vague. I introduced the SIMple goal concept in *One Page Talent Management* to help make goal setting easier and more focused. The initials S-I-M in SIMple stand for:

- Specific. Describe your promise in ten words or less. "Complete the Corn Crunchers product launch by February 1," "Reduce cycle time on machine one by 20 percent," or "Increase average private client account balance by $100,000." Remember that each is the entire goal statement; there aren't ten bullets underneath listing subgoals.

- Important. Each promise should help the organization to deliver one of its most important objectives. Don't include trivial goals or big tasks. If you limit yourself to three goals, it's much easier to ensure each is important to the organization.

- Measurable. There must be a way to assess whether you've achieved, exceeded, or fallen short of the goal. Quantitative goals are the easiest to measure, but many people work on projects or processes where the best measure is the quality or acceptance of the output. In those cases, you can measure by customer perceptions, sales, your manager's assessment, being on time, successful delivery, and so on.

Get Coached

With fewer, bigger, aligned, well-written goals in place, you're positioned to deliver great results. You will find it easier to achieve those goals if you get clear direction and honest correction as you work on them. The ideal amount of coaching is similar to the spoken driving directions on your phone. You get guidance before a critical turn that tells you to be ready and where to exit. You are rerouted if you go offtrack. It's not a steady stream of information, just the right directions delivered when they're most needed.

You may have a manager who's great at coaching you on your performance. She conducts regular check-ins, provides transparent direction, and encourages you when she sees progress. If not, you can ask your manager for a radically simple coaching approach to use with you. I created 2+2 coaching to make it easier to get regular, specific, and helpful advice to improve your performance. 2+2 coaching gives you just enough correction and direction to ensure you're on target to achieve your goal. It's easy and nonthreatening for your manager to deliver, and it works so well that some of the world's largest companies use 2+2 to coach their employees.

In 2+2 coaching, you ask your manager to spend fifteen minutes with you (it can be more if you or they prefer) every three months for a conversation that includes two topics:

- Two comments about your progress on your promises. I don't mean two comments on every promise, but two for all three promises. What are the most important observations or advice she has for you? This could be, "Rajan, the new hand-soap product launch seems to be going quite well. We're ahead of schedule and the project team tells me that you're a strong and inspirational leader. Great job! On the marketing strategy, based on your progress, it feels as if this is not your priority, even though it's one of your three promises. I'd like to see a draft of that within thirty days. Let me know what I can do to help you get there." The goal of her two comments is to make sure that you both are aligned about your progress.

- Two "feedforward" comments to enhance your performance or behaviors. We often think that feedback is the right path to improvement, but the simple, powerful concept of "feedforward" is based on the science that says our brains often reject feedback that doesn't reinforce our self-image.[7] Feedforward provides the exact same direction but without the backward-looking critique.[8] To contrast the two approaches, feedback might sound like, "Suzie, your presentation in the executive team meeting last week was too long. Can you please tighten those up in the future?" Since you can't change what you've done in the past, it's frustrating to be criticized for it and you may not change your behavior. A feedforward 2+2 statement from your manager would be, "Suzie, the executive team has asked that presentations to them be brief and focused on the few most important points. As you prepare for next week's meeting, please make sure your presentation has the key facts presented early and can be finished within ten minutes." When you hear feedforward advice, you still get specific guidance for how to improve, but without being criticized for things that have already happened. You'll learn more about the feedforward technique in step two, "behave to perform."

You can suggest to your manager that he or she use 2+2 coaching (see the resources in the appendix and at www.the8steps.com). Or, set quarterly meetings with him where you ask him those questions.

Wrapping Up

High performance starts with great delivery driven by big goals and transparent coaching. Big goals create focus and motivation. Coaching ensures you're on the shortest path to success. Big goals and coaching are also a great place to recognize that you need to take personal accountability to do both things well. Your manager may not be expert at those activities, but that shouldn't hold you back from being a high performer.

Now that you have the right goals in place and a plan for coaching, you're on the path to higher performance. It's time to take step two and build the behaviors that differentiate great performers from merely good ones.

What Can Get in the Way

- My manager sets my goals for me. How can I better control the process? That's fine. Review those goals and suggest changes to your manager if the goals aren't fewer, bigger, and aligned or don't meet the SIMple criteria.

- My job is routine; I do the same things each day. How can I set a goal that improves what I deliver? In any job, you can improve the cost, quality, or speed of what you do. If you do analysis and produce reports, can you do that faster or with more valuable insights? If you're the receptionist, list the five things you do most days and pick the one that you can most improve. Anything that you do can be done better.

- **My manager insists that I have more than three goals.** That's not uncommon; he may be using goal setting as a substitute for project management. Let him know that you want to focus on the most important things, tell him the three goals you believe are the most important, and ask if he agrees. Even if you end up having to list five, eight, ten, or more goals as part of your company's process, you'll understand which of them are most important.

- **My manager isn't an expert in goal setting.** Most managers aren't, because they only do goal setting once a year and most have never been taught the proper approach. Share this book (or its core principles) and let them know that there are more resources at www.the8steps.com.

- **How do I get credit for doing my day job if it's not in my goals?** You get credit for doing your day job through your regular paycheck. Goals exist to focus your efforts and energy to achieve something above and beyond what you typically do.

- **My goals change all the time during the year. It's difficult to know what to work on.** While it's not unusual for changing priorities to occasionally shift your focus, if your goals change every quarter, they are probably set too low. Check whether they meet the definition of a larger promise or if they sound more like activities. A promise shouldn't change very often, even if some of the tactics required to achieve it do.

- **What if I set big goals and fail?** That's where high performers separate themselves from others. High performers want to take appropriate risks to prove that they can overachieve. On occasion, you will fall short of a goal. You will, over time, deliver more great results than your peers and be recognized as a high performer.

Remember and Apply

The conclusive science says:

- Goals matter. You'll perform better if you have them.

- Fewer, bigger goals will improve your performance and help you focus on what really matters.

- Get regular feedforward coaching to guide your efforts in the right direction.

You should:

- Create your three big promises that will differentiate you as a high performer.

- Eliminate tactical activities from your goals; move them to a project plan.

- Ask your manager to regularly use 2+2 coaching with you to ensure you're on the path to high performance on your goals.

Try using:

- Goal-setting form in the appendix

Step 2

Behave to Perform

There's plenty of bad information, folk wisdom, and sketchy advice about which behaviors will make you a high performer. One of the biggest myths is that having good "leadership behaviors" is what matters most. Science, practice, and the history of two Silicon Valley visionaries tell a more nuanced story.

A Tale of Two Founders

In 2000, Yahoo! was six years old, valued at $125 billion, and one the world's most popular internet portals. Founded in 1994 by Stanford graduate students Jerry Yang and David Filo as a guide to their favorite internet sites, it quickly transformed into an essential front door to the internet. The environment for search engines was competitive, but Yahoo! was well positioned, well staffed, and well funded to win. Google was just eighteen months old.

Cofounder Jerry Yang was often described as a "nice guy"—someone who cried when he had to announce the company's first round of layoffs, was quiet, and was fiercely loyal to his fellow Yahoos. There's nothing wrong with being labeled "nice," but those who called him that often intended that adjective as a slight, not a compliment. Referring to Yang's unwillingness to fight tougher against Google, billionaire entrepreneur Mark Cuban said, "Jerry's too nice a guy. He cares too much. Sometimes, when a competitor like Google comes along, you've got to get mean and you've got to get tough."[1] Other observers offered similar comments about Yang's style.[2]

That same year, Apple Computer's renaissance was in full swing, as sales strengthened for its jelly-bean-shaped, brightly colored iMac, and the company emerged as a force in design and technology. Led by founder and once-again CEO Steve Jobs, Apple's stock price had increased more than 300 percent from the iMac launch and more than 1,000 percent since Jobs's return in 1997. Apple was positioned for, but hardly guaranteed, success. In late 2000, some pricing missteps by the company and a general slowing of the technology market produced Apple's first unprofitable quarter in three years.

Apple employees experienced Jobs as a mercurial, demanding, abusive, and manipulative leader. He used profanity to emphasize his points and regularly brought employees to tears. His biographer, Walter Isaacson, said about Jobs, "He's not warm and fuzzy... He was not the world's greatest manager. In fact, he could have been one of the world's worst managers."[3]

Ten years later, Jobs ruled a company that had fundamentally redefined how people interact with technology, listen to music, and access information. He had evolved into an iconic CEO and arguably the leading entrepreneur of his generation. In 2018, eight years after Jobs's death from pancreatic cancer, Apple had a market value of more than $900 billion and was the world's most valuable publicly traded company.

At Yahoo!, Yang paid the price for being nice. A 2008 report discussing Yahoo's future said the "mandate for the new CEO, whoever he or she is? Fire people. Specifically, make the harsh decisions Jerry has been unwilling to make because he's too close to the company and too nice a guy." The board fired Yang as CEO later that year, and he stayed on as chief Yahoo! until he left the company in 2012. He was widely derided for refusing a buyout offer from Microsoft in 2008 that valued Yahoo! at 62 percent above its market price. In 2017, Verizon purchased Yahoo! for $4.5 billion, 10 percent of what Microsoft had offered for it nine years earlier and about 0.5 percent the market value of Apple.[4]

In this story of two founders, it's difficult to prove that Yang being too nice and Jobs being quite mean influenced their companies' direction. But it begs an important and oft-asked question: Do nice people or their mean counterparts finish first? The science says it doesn't hurt to be nice, but that there's no guarantee that you will be more successful if you behave like a stereotypical good leader or that it will hold you back if you behave more aggressively.

Why It Matters

Behaviors help you differentiate yourself as a high performer because they prove that you can do more than just get things done. They're responsible for 15 percent to 40 percent of your total performance, depending on your role.[5] Your company also thinks behaviors are a big deal—86 percent of companies measure behaviors in their performance management process.[6] These behaviors may or may not be what actually drives performance, but they signal what your leaders pay attention to. More importantly, you can assume that everyone you work with evaluates your behaviors every day and interacts with you based on their impressions. How they perceive your behavior feeds the office gossip pool and influences your performance, network, image, and ultimately, success.

High performers work hard to identify the most productive behaviors, learn new behaviors where needed, and stop showing the less helpful ones. It's challenging to differentiate which behaviors matter, since thousands of books, consultants, blogs, and webinars claim to tell you how successful people behave. You're fortunate that there's great science that tells you which behaviors will make you a great people leader, able to inspire change, or drive big results. The challenge is that what makes you successful at one of those things may make you less successful at another. That's why step two to high performance is to know how you behave today and which behaviors will make you successful tomorrow.

How It Works

The science about how behavior drives performance says that you'll be a higher performer if you:

- Understand yourself. You know how you typically behave and how that affects your performance.[7]

- Choose the right behaviors. You know which behaviors are most likely to make you a high performer.[8]

- Adapt quickly. You know how to quickly and easily show performance-driving behaviors.[9]

Understand Yourself

The way you behave is a combination of how your personality guides you to behave and how you choose to behave. Your personality strongly influences your behaviors, but it doesn't control them. You've learned over time to show other behaviors that will make you a better performer, peer, or manager, even if they're inconsistent with your core personality. When people interact with you, they see a mix of the behaviors your personality wants you to show and the behaviors that you consciously choose to show (see figure 2-1).

If that's confusing, think of your personality as similar to the natural hair on your head. You're born with hair that's a certain

FIGURE 2-1

How others see you

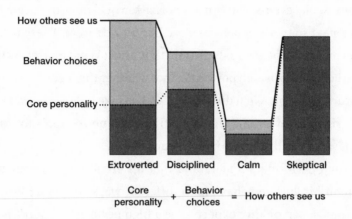

color and thickness that naturally falls a certain way. Just like personality, your natural hair is about 50 percent inherited from your parents, and that influence will always affect its appearance.[10] However, as you grew up, you decided that you preferred your hair in a different style, color, or length. You may now spend a significant amount of time and effort to make your hair appear different from its natural state. It's still your hair, but you've chosen to present a stylized version of it to friends, family, and coworkers.

That stylized version of your hair represents the image you want others to see. It also isn't the natural you. Wash your hair, get rid of the gel or color, and the "pure" you is back. Your personality and behaviors work the same way. Personality is largely set by your late teens, and it will forever strongly guide how you behave.[11] But you can stylize your behaviors in any way you choose to present the image you want. That's why personality psychologists laugh when they hear people say, "I can't change; this is just how I am."

The most important takeaway from step two is that you control your behaviors. If you're a little edgy in meetings, you can smile more and ask questions to understand another's point of view, rather than reacting too quickly to their comments. If you're very shy at social events, you can memorize ten questions to ask anyone you meet so that you behave more like an extrovert. These behaviors might not be the real you, and that's fine. What matters is that you behave like a high performer, not whether that behavior comes naturally to you. We'll discuss in step six, fake it, how you can fake the right behavior and that sometimes it's more important to do that successfully than to be the genuine you.

High performers understand that different parts of your personality influence behaviors in different ways. You don't have to become a personality expert to be a high performer, but it's helpful to know that there are five parts of your personality (typically called the "Big 5") and that some parts matter much more to performance than others. These Big 5 form the foundation of what science knows about personality—thoroughly tested and proven. Table 2-1 shows the five areas and what the science says about how much each influences your performance at work.

Your personality influences your behavior enough that it's helpful to understand where you score on each factor. If you're low in certain areas, it suggests that you'll need to consistently work harder than others to show those behaviors. You can get a rough indication of your personality traits with a quick assessment (see table 2-2). A valid, fast, and thorough personality assessment (Ten-Item Personality Inventory) can be found in the appendix.

Conscientiousness is the personality factor that most influences your performance; it's twice as powerful as any other factor. If you're naturally wired to focus on results, be disciplined, and pursue tasks, you're likely to be a higher performer than someone who must work hard to ignore distractions and force themselves to buckle down. Emotional stability is slightly helpful in every

TABLE 2-1

Your five personality factors

The Big 5 personality factors	More of the factor means you show more of these behaviors*	How much it matters to high performance at work
Conscientiousness	Dependable, thorough, hardworking, persevering, organized, a planner	A moderate amount, in every job
Emotional stability	Calm, steady, self-confident, low anxiety, upbeat	A little, in every job
Extroversion	Sociable, gregarious, talkative, assertive, active, ambitious	A little helpful in sales and customer service roles; uncertain impact in managerial roles
Agreeableness	Courteous, flexible, cooperative, forgiving, soft-hearted, tolerant	A little if you're in a customer service role; may hurt performance in managerial roles
Openness to experience	Imaginative, cultured, curious, original, broad-minded, artistically oriented	None

*Robert Hogan, Gordon J. Curphy, and Joyce Hogan, "What We Know about Leadership: Effectiveness and Personality," *American Psychologist* 49, no. 6 (1994): 493.

TABLE 2-2

Five-factor assessment

Read the adjectives in the behaviors column in table 2-1. On a scale of 1 to 5, 5 being "this perfectly describes me" to 1 being "this does not describe me at all," rate yourself below.

Conscientiousness	Emotional stability	Extroversion	Agreeableness	Openness to experience

role, for an obvious reason—people want to interact with you more when you're predictable and calm.

The other personality factors may seem as if they should help performance. Shouldn't openness to experience help you to think more creatively or be a better risk taker or value diversity? It may lead to any of those, but there's no proof that more of those things lead to higher performance. Similarly, we may think that more agreeableness will make for a much nicer manager. It will. But that nice manager with high agreeableness will be less likely to confront bosses, give direct feedback to their team, or make tough calls on people and projects.

If you're higher or lower on these factors, it's helpful to understand how your personality naturally pulls you in certain directions. If you're low on conscientiousness, you might need to create project plans, calendars, lists, or other tools to help you to stay focused on tasks. If you're high on agreeableness, you may want to ask others if you're making tough enough decisions on people and projects.

Choose the Right Behaviors

Now that you know how your personality might influence your behavior, it's time to understand which behaviors best predict high performance. Before we do this, let's assume the basics. You are likely ethical, honest, and fair; you don't scream at your employees, steal, lie (big ones, at least), or cheat. You may think that's an obvious baseline for behaviors, but if you consider how many people don't demonstrate the basics, you'll understand why I start with this. If you violate these baseline behaviors, you will never be a sustained high performer—period. Any temporary success you gain from bad behaviors will pale in comparison to the shame of getting caught, getting fired, or going to jail.

With that baseline established, let's start with the good news and bad news from the science. The good news is that research tells you which behaviors should make you a higher performer. The bad news is that the behaviors that matter change, depending on how you define performance. We know from personality science that some behaviors (task focused, committed to getting things done, calm, confident) create higher performance in almost every situation. But what other behaviors matter and when?

BEHAVIOR OPTION #1: BEHAVE LIKE A TRANSFORMATIONAL LEADER. A model called transformational leadership describes behaviors that are thoroughly tested and well proven to create high performance. Transformational behaviors help ensure you're well thought of by those around you and that you focus on results.[12] You can be confident that transformational leader behaviors are science based and accurate, since the model has been studied, tested, and validated in hundreds of real-world experiments.

Don't be thrown by the label. You don't need to be transforming something or be a leader for these behaviors to apply. People who behave as transformational leaders are consistently rated higher on their team's motivation, satisfaction, and their own leadership effectiveness than those who lead in any other way.[13] Even if you're not managing people, the behaviors still apply. Display them to your peers and superiors to get the same benefits.

Transformational leaders do four things well:[14]

- Connect: Show genuine concern for employees; they're able to personally connect with them even if they don't directly manage them.

- Innovate: Push their team to create novel solutions and take risks.

- Inspire: Offer a compelling vision and encourage employees to perform at higher levels.

- Model: Act consistently with their vision and the goals they've set for others.

Along with being time tested, transformational leadership behaviors aren't very influenced by your core personality, so no one has a natural advantage over you in being a transformational leader.[15]

If you need to pull others along with you, transformational leadership is a great model. If you need to push them forward, you may want to consider the science about being a performance driver.

BEHAVIOR OPTION #2: BEHAVE LIKE A PERFORMANCE DRIVER. You're on the hottest of performance hot seats If you're the CEO of a company owned by a private equity (PE) or venture capital (VC) firm. Those PE and VC firms have put their money into your company and want a lot more of it back, and quickly. It's fair to say that CEOs of PE- or VC-owned companies are under more constant performance pressure than almost any leader in any other situation.

The behaviors that work in that heated, performance-obsessed environment were identified in a study that assessed 316 CEO candidates for PE- and VC-owned companies on thirty different characteristics that might predict high performance. It found that those thirty characteristics naturally fell into two categories—general ability (aggressive, persistent, proactive, etc.) and interpersonal (team player, open to criticism, etc.). In short, one category was about getting things done, and one category was about working well with others (see table 2-3).

In this study, the CEO candidates could be rated from high to low in each category, so the categories weren't mutually exclusive.

TABLE 2-3

Which behaviors do performance-driving CEOs show?

General ability (mattered)	Interpersonal (didn't matter)
Fast	Respectful
Aggressive	Open to criticism
Persistent	Good listening skills
Efficient	Teamwork
Proactive	
High standards	

When the scientists looked at the company performance of the CEOs who got the jobs, they found that the most successful CEOs were high on general ability and low on interpersonal. Yes, true to stereotype, CEOs who were hard-driving and not particularly strong on the soft stuff were the highest performers.[16]

What's interesting is that the behaviors in the general-ability category sound very much like the ones that define the personality factor of conscientiousness and are scientifically proven to improve performance. The interpersonal behaviors bear a strong resemblance to the personality factors openness to experience and agreeableness that typically have little effect on work performance.

This finding does not give you permission to act like a jerk, but it shows that there are different paths to high performance. The key point to remember is that the study was about CEOs—a group at the top of the organizational pyramid. They're likely far less concerned that they get along with others and far more concerned they get stuff done. They know that few PE firms will give them credit for being a great leader, so it's not surprising that the adage, "What gets measured is what gets done" applies. If you're not already at the top, I'd suggest that both great results and great interpersonal behaviors are essential ingredients for high performance.

Adapt Quickly

If behaviors are your secret weapon for high performance, the first step is to know how well armed you are. Are your behaviors consistent with your preferred model? Do you have any derailing behaviors that will likely throw you offtrack? High performers want to know, even if the answers may be a bit painful.

The "Ten-Item Personality Inventory" in the appendix can help you better understand your natural tendencies. What matters more is how your boss, coworkers, and direct reports perceive your behaviors. Their perception should matter to you, because other people's opinions, not your own, will decide if you're considered a high performer.

You should also care about what others think because your view of your performance and behaviors is the least accurate one. Everyone around us sees us more accurately than we see ourselves. That's because we're all wonderfully delusional about our own capabilities and behaviors, and the less capable we are, the more delusional we are. There's even a phenomenon called the Dunning-Kruger effect showing that the least competent people are the least aware that they are incompetent. They're even more convinced than their smarter peers that their opinions are correct.[17]

There are two ways to find out how others perceive us—ask them directly or ask them indirectly.

ASK DIRECTLY. Asking others directly about your performance and behaviors isn't as scary as it sounds. Start with the mindset that everyone can get better at something. The people you ask for feedback and advice have their own list of self-improvement to-dos. You're just getting to your list first.

Your goal when you ask someone directly is to get a suggestion or two for how to behave even better, not to get a comprehensive assessment of you. Here's the easy way, courtesy of Marshall Goldsmith, the best-selling author of *What Got You Here Won't Get You There*.

An approach called "feedforward" makes others comfortable giving you insights about what to change and makes you feel comfortable receiving them.[18] In feedforward, you ask a few people you trust how you can be a higher performer in the future. This can be as simple as saying, "Hi, Mary, I just read this new book called the *8 Steps to High Performance*. It says you should ask some people you know well for one idea about how to perform even better going forward. This isn't feedback about the past, but a suggestion for what I should start, stop, or continue doing to improve. What one suggestion do you have for me about what I should start, stop, or continue to do to be a higher performer?"

To make that simple process work best:

- Use it with people who you know well. Ask people who know you relatively well and who will feel comfortable sharing their thoughts. This can include close colleagues, direct reports, your boss, or anyone else who's worked with you long enough to know your strengths and what you should improve.

- Don't surprise them with the question. Ask them over a cup of coffee or as part of another conversation. Send them an email that explains why you're asking and what you'll do with their answers. Don't ambush them by sticking your head into their cubicle or office and demanding that they share their insights.

- Follow up. You don't have to act on every suggestion you receive, but a few will likely be worth a try. Once you try them and see great results, follow up with the person who provided that advice. Let them know that you tried their suggestion and it worked. Thank them again for their help. If you do this, they'll be more open to giving you insights in the future, which will further improve your performance and start a virtuous cycle.

ASK INDIRECTLY. If the direct approach seems too scary or difficult to pull off, use the indirect approach of a 360-degree assessment to get similar insights. In a typical 360-degree assessment process, your manager, some peers, some direct reports, and possibly a few others rate you on a set of behaviors. They may rate you as being good or bad at those behaviors or assess how frequently you show them. They may provide the same type of feedforward advice mentioned. Their answers will be combined (anonymously) into a report that summarizes their assessment of you and possibly compares the scores against some reference or benchmark. When you get this report back, keep in mind that we can each get better at something. You shouldn't be embarrassed, regardless of what the report says, because you now know the facts and can decide which behaviors you want to change. If you want to be a high performer, it's far better to get these insights now than to find out only when your career or performance stalls. Also, the people you work with are telling you, "Here are things that limit your ability to be a high performer." You can choose to accept or ignore their opinions, but if you want to perform close to your theoretical maximum, it's an easy choice.

The next step is what separates those who improve from those who don't. It can be both challenging and humbling. Before you take this step, remember that everyone around you already knows how you behave and wants some of those behaviors to change. They've given you specific advice about how to change. If you ignore their feedback, do you think they'll have a more positive or more negative impression of you?

To show your commitment, set up a one-on-one meeting or call with each person you invited to give feedback (it doesn't matter if they participated). In your invitation, tell them that you'll use this meeting to share your action plan and ask for their advice. In the meeting, say:

- **What you did.** "I recently went through a 360-degree assessment process to help ensure I'm a strong performer. I don't know who participated, so I'm meeting with everyone who was invited so I can share my action plan and get any additional advice you may have for me."

- **What you heard.** "There was a lot of helpful information in the report about things I do well and things I need to improve. I was pleased to hear that people think [list two or three positive findings from the 360]. I also heard that people would like me to be better at [list two or three improvement areas]."

- **What your plan is.** "Based on that information, I've developed an action plan for how I will improve. I wanted to share it with you and get any other advice you have for me." (Briefly describe the two or three steps you plan to take toward two or three areas for change.)

- **What's their advice?** "Do you have other suggestions for how I can improve in the areas I mentioned?" (Don't argue with, critique, or dismiss any suggestion they offer. Ask questions if you need to understand their suggestion.)

When you've finished listening, just say thank you.

You should ask your manager or your human resource representative if your company offers a 360-degree assessment process and how to participate in it. If you're in a smaller company without a human resource group, see the resources in the appendix.

Which Behaviors Can Hurt You

When we discuss behaviors, we care about both those that can help your performance and those that can hurt it. Imagine if, when you were starting your career, someone had said to you, "I can tell you today exactly how you will hurt your performance in the future—not just this year, but ten years, twenty years, thirty years from now. And, I can tell you how to avoid making those mistakes." Would you listen to what that person had to say?

One of this book's most powerful insights, and one that's guaranteed to make you a higher performer, is that it's possible to predict which behaviors will harm your performance. With this information, you can avoid showing the behaviors that will otherwise undercut your success.

You know that some behaviors are likely to give you a performance advantage. Those same behaviors can hurt your performance if they're turned up too high and become overdone strengths. When that happens, those behaviors become "derailers." Derailers are your natural, unstyled hair—messy, disheveled, and perhaps a bit scary. Anytime you forget to show the stylized you, your derailers can come out. That's most likely to happen when you're tired, when you've let your guard down around friends, or when you're under stress.

These derailing behaviors might have served you well over time, but now they're an anchor that drags behind you and slows your progress. Consider a tenacious marketing leader who quickly advanced by designing highly creative marketing campaigns and aggressively pushing her ideas in a "boy's club" environment. She rightfully believes she has excellent ideas and is always ready to defend them. When she is promoted to the company's head of marketing, those strengths show up very differently—as derailers. Her pride in her own ideas means she often overrides her team with her preferred concepts, which reduces her team members' motivation to innovate and take risks. Her strong advocacy, which allowed her to emerge as a leader, is now perceived by some executive team peers as defensiveness and unwillingness to compromise.

That supply chain leader who brilliantly builds relationships across the company? His boss and other senior leaders love him. He has great political instincts and is successful partly because he's very good at managing up. Because he values those senior-level relationships, when he's under stress he hesitates to make decisions or makes the choice he knows his boss prefers. This causes his team members to feel that he doesn't back them when needed. He's not going to take risks, because those might make him or his boss look bad, and his lack of risk taking will quickly plateau his career.

Those behaviors are called derailers for obvious reasons— you'll go off the tracks if you show them too often. Everyone has derailers, including high performers, so the secret is to recognize which ones you have and work hard to keep them in check. This is also a key reason not to focus on your strengths when you plan your development. If you overemphasize your strengths, they can become derailers.

There are eleven different ways our behaviors can derail our performance, according to legendary personality scientist Robert Hogan and his firm, Hogan Assessments (see table 2-4). Hogan has created a quick and easy assessment of derailers exclusively for readers of 8 Steps. You can use this assessment to better understand your potential derailers and what will happen if you don't correct them (table 2-5).

TABLE 2-4

The eleven derailers

Excitable: Being overly enthusiastic about, and then disappointed with, people or projects
- Consequence: Seems to lack persistence.

Skeptical: Being socially insightful, but cynical and overly sensitive to criticism.
- Consequence: Seems to lack trust.

Cautious: Being overly worried about being criticized.
- Consequence: Seems resistant to change and reluctant to take chances.

Reserved: Lacking interest in or awareness of the feelings of others.
- Consequence: Seems to be a poor communicator.

Leisurely: Being independent, ignoring others' requests, and becoming irritable if they persist.
- Consequence: Seems stubborn, procrastinating, and uncooperative.

Bold: Having inflated views of one's competency and worth.
- Consequence: Seems unable to admit mistakes or learn from experience.

Mischievous: Being charming, risk taking, and excitement seeking.
- Consequence: Seems to have trouble maintaining commitments and learning from experience.

Colorful: Being dramatic, engaging, and attention seeking.
- Consequence: Seems preoccupied with being noticed and may lack sustained focus.

Imaginative: Thinking and acting in interesting, unusual, and even eccentric ways.
- Consequence: Seems creative but possibly lacking in judgment.

Diligent: Being conscientious, a perfectionist, hard to please.
- Consequence: Tends to disempower staff.

Dutiful: Being eager to please and reluctant to act independently.
- Consequence: Tends to be pleasant and agreeable, but reluctant to support subordinates.

Source: Hogan Assessment Systems, Hogan Developmental Survey, 2009.

Follow the instructions in table 2-5 to roughly understand your potential derailers and refer back to table 2-4 to see the consequences of each.

To avoid your derailers, you must recognize which ones you're most likely to show and prevent yourself from exhibiting them. You can use the feedback or feedforward approach to find out which derailers you typically show. The appendix includes more tools to help you more precisely identify and neutralize your derailers.

TABLE 2-5

Derailer mini-assessment

Instructions: For each of the statements listed below, mark whether the statement generally describes you (Y) or does not (N).

1. **Excitable:** I have been so frustrated with projects that I gave up.
2. **Skeptical:** I know who my enemies are.
3. **Cautious:** I live by the rule "better safe than sorry."
4. **Reserved:** I like to keep people guessing about my intentions.
5. **Leisurely:** I am smarter than my boss.
6. **Bold:** Someday people will appreciate my talent.
7. **Colorful:** I enjoy being the life of the party.
8. **Mischievous:** I can persuade others to do almost anything.
9. **Imaginative:** Others are often amazed by my creativity.
10. **Diligent:** I tend to be a perfectionist.
11. **Dutiful:** I take pride in being a good organizational citizen.

Scoring: If you answered a question with a Y, it's likely that you'll show this derailer to others at least periodically.

Source: Developed by Dr. Robert Hogan, founder, Hogan Assessments, exclusively for use in *8 Steps to High Performance*. Copyright Hogan Assessments. No use without explicit permission.

Make Behaviors Work in Your Company

We've discussed two key behavioral models, but many companies have their own model (leadership model, values model) to help rate your performance, plan your development, or assess your capabilities. That model is your company's statement that certain behaviors matter more there than others. You should care about these behaviors because your company cares about them, but consider them with these two questions in mind:

- How important are these behaviors to your ultimate success? Just because this behavior model exists and is listed in your performance evaluation doesn't mean it will affect your success. You should care most about the behaviors that affect your pay, your performance rating, or your ability to move forward in the company. The easiest way to understand that is to see if the behaviors are part of your company's performance management process or talent review and succession planning process.

- **Which behaviors matter most?** The other possibility is that a few behaviors in your company's behavior model matter more than others. The best way to find out is to ask your manager questions such as: Which three behaviors in this model matter most? Which behaviors does the CEO care most about? Which behaviors do high-potential leaders here show to you most frequently? Your goal is to know where to focus your energy and efforts. Remember, you get promoted because you deliver great results and perform well on the behaviors the company cares about most.

Wrapping Up

Understanding and displaying the behaviors that drive high performance may seem challenging. After all, there are hundreds of possible behaviors that your direct reports, peers, and boss might want you to show. Relax. There are only three things that you need to do: Understand how you're naturally wired to behave and how people see you behave today. Identify which few behaviors are most important for your success at work. Develop an action plan to adapt quickly to those behaviors.

Your completion of steps one and two means that you can now deliver big results, while displaying high-performer behaviors. That's the core of high performance, but it doesn't guarantee success. You must continue to grow these capabilities to compete with those who want to outperform you. Step three, "grow yourself faster," tells you how.

What Can Get in the Way

- My company doesn't have a behavior model. What should I use to guide my behaviors? Ask your manager which three behaviors will make you a high performer or start with the transformational leader or performance driver models described earlier in this chapter.

- My manager says one thing about which behaviors matter and my company says something else. Who should I believe? If the company's behavior model is used to determine your performance, help you develop, or assess you for promotion, then that's the model to follow. If not, check with a few trusted colleagues who know your company's culture well. Ask if they think your manager's view captures the behaviors that truly matter. Your manager may know the secret path to success or may just have a strong opinion about what's right.

- Behaviors don't matter at my company. People behave badly and/or behaviors aren't included in our performance management or succession processes. Just because behaviors aren't hardwired into your company's practices doesn't mean that they don't matter. Your company culture will send strong signals about which behaviors matter most. Ask your manager and/or few people you consider high performers for their opinion about which behaviors high performers in your company show.

    The person you see behaving badly may be delivering such strong results that the company is giving them a temporary pass on certain behaviors. Alternatively, others might not see the same behaviors as you do, or the company might fire that person tomorrow. Your best strategy is to understand and demonstrate the behaviors that matter most to your performance.

- The behaviors in my company model don't align with my values. There's an easy choice to make in the rare event that the behaviors your company wants you to show are fundamentally different from your personal values. Unless you're the CEO, you have little influence over those behaviors, so either adapt to what your company prefers or find a new employer where its values and yours are better aligned.

- We have a new CEO (or regional leader or district leader) who is asking for a different set of behaviors than our old CEO. During your career, you'll have many bosses with many opinions about the right way to behave. Hopefully their views won't be so radically different that they give you behavior whiplash. As long as their behaviors are relatively consistent with what the company requires, it makes sense to adapt.

- How can I fix my derailers? Since your derailers are a part of your core personality, you can't permanently fix them, but you can learn to recognize and control them. For example, you may know that one of your derailers is your skepticism. That derailer can cause you to challenge others' facts, doubt their true intentions, and come across as cynical.

    If you're in a meeting where someone presents an analysis you disagree with, your natural tendency may be to instantly challenge their facts or analytical ability. If you know about your derailers, when you hear facts you think are incorrect, say, "Can you tell me more about why you chose those data sources and how you did your analysis?" or "Are there other conclusions you could draw from that same data?"

- I don't respect everyone's opinion equally. Do I have to ask everyone for their views on my behavior? No. You're more likely to act on feedback from people you respect. The danger is that if you only select people for feedback or feedforward who agree with your view of yourself, you may miss insights that could help you be a higher performer.

Remember and Apply

The conclusive science says:

- Your personality provides a baseline for your behaviors but not an excuse; you control how you behave.

- You can predict which behaviors are likely to derail your career and start to correct them today.

- Some people are born with personality characteristics that give them a natural performance advantage in some situations.

You should:

- Understand your baseline personality and how you're naturally oriented to behave.

- Identify which behaviors are most important for your success in your current environment and list the three specific activities it will take to improve them.

- Know your derailers and have a plan to recognize when they might show and how to keep them hidden.

Try using:

- Ten-item personality inventory (in the appendix)

- Derailer mini-assessment (table 2-5)

Step 3

Grow
Yourself
Faster

In September 2010, billionaire entrepreneur and PayPal cofounder Peter Thiel said something that caused middle-class parents to cover their children's ears and Ivy League deans to recoil in horror. Thiel suggested that smart kids might not benefit from attending college and questioned the entire value of formal higher education. He then backed up his statement by announcing the Thiel Fellowship—a $100,000, two-year grant to students who choose not to attend college so that they can pursue their entrepreneurial dreams.[1]

The annual selection process for Thiel Fellows is incredibly rigorous, with just twenty to twenty-five future fellows accepted representing less than 1 percent of the total applicants.[2] Harvard University, in comparison, accepts about 5 percent of those who apply for its four-year, more than $250,000, undergraduate education.[3] Once selected, Thiel Fellows are free to pursue their goals, whether that involves building the next Google, conducting scientific research, or creating a social movement. They get counseling, networking, and the invaluable label of Thiel Fellow.

Thiel's announcement caused the higher education bureaucracy to convulse, with former Harvard University president Larry Summers saying, "I think the single most misdirected bit of philanthropy in this decade is Peter Thiel's special program to bribe people to drop out of college."[4] The argument against Thiel's approach is that successful college dropouts like Microsoft founder Bill Gates and Facebook founder Mark Zuckerberg are the exception, not the norm. Its detractors say it's unlikely that other young minds would benefit from pursuing a similar path and that those without four-year college degrees earn about $24,000 less annually than college graduates.[5]

The Thiel versus Summers debate raises an interesting question for anyone who wants to be a high performer: What's the fastest, surest way to successfully grow?

Why It Matters

You compete every day against every individual in your company or industry who wants to be a high performer. If you grow more capabilities more quickly than they do, you'll perform better today and earn more opportunities to perform better in the future. Those opportunities will make you even more skilled and attract more new learning opportunities, and a virtuous cycle will take hold. If you effectively apply your new learnings, you'll advance faster and more successfully than your peers. That's an ideal way to quickly approach your theoretical maximum performance.

Also, most executives understand that better-quality talent delivers better business results. They'll search for that rare talent, pay them well, and give them more opportunities to continue their development. When you grow, you get a better choice of jobs and more money in your pocket. Every minute you aren't growing your capabilities, you're losing your competitive advantage to someone who's working hard to grow theirs. That's why "grow yourself faster" is step three to high performance.

What We Know

The great news about growing is that you have a lot of control over how much and how fast you grow. The more you grow in the right areas, the more likely you are to be a high performer. When you grow, you build crystallized intelligence—more useful content in your brain—giving you more facts, insights, and observations that you can use to deliver better results.

The research is clear about how we grow. All you need to remember is the mantra "70/20/10." That research-derived mantra says that roughly 70 percent of your professional growth will come from the work experiences you have, 20 percent will come from your interactions with others, and 10 percent will come from formal education (see figure 3-1). The 70/20/10 ratio also reflects the process that many successful leaders have used to build their careers.[6]

These percentages also make intuitive sense, because if formal learning were a larger part of the model, you'd study a lot but never get practice. If feedback were a larger part, you'd spend too much time hearing what you did wrong and not enough time practicing to get better. That 70 percent experience versus 10 percent education balance may be one reason Thiel suggested that bright young people should focus on getting experiences rather than earning a four-year degree.

Some people argue that the 70/20/10 ratio undervalues learning, because only 10 percent is devoted to it. My response is that

FIGURE 3-1

How you grow

Activity	How it helps
70% meaningful, challenging experiences	Tests and grows your capabilities
20% coaching, observing, and feedback	Provides guidance for how to develop or improve performance and behaviors
10% formal learning in classrooms and courses	Provides structured learning of skills, frameworks, and ideas

I'm very glad that my personal physician went to four years of medical school to learn his craft. But, it was his twenty years of experience after his education that made him a great physician. I don't mean that formal education isn't important. But, you should consider which levers will most quickly make you a higher performer. Education that may seem critical to success often isn't. Only thirty-nine *Fortune* 100 CEOs have an MBA, and many of those leaders didn't earn them at top-ranked schools.[7]

Grow Faster

Think of growth as a cycle—perform, get feedback, perform again better (see the learning cycle in figure 3-2). The faster and more often you move through that cycle, the faster you'll develop and get the next opportunity to learn a new skill, test a new behavior, and get more helpful feedback. Each cycle you move through should make you more competent and more competitive.

To grow faster, you must understand which development activities matter most and do as many of them as quickly as possible. Few people manage their own careers with this level of purpose

FIGURE 3-2

The learning cycle

and discipline. You need to be very clear about your desired destination on that development journey—an obvious item that's often missing from a development plan. The three steps to grow faster are:

1. Determine your from/to.

2. Get the experiences and create a personal experience map.

3. Get feedback and feedforward on your capabilities and behaviors.

1. Determine Your From/To

If you want driving directions from Google Maps, Google asks you to provide two pieces of information—your current location and your desired location. The more precisely you enter each coordinate, the more confident you'll be that you'll get where you want to go. If you enter "East Coast, USA" as your current location and "West Coast, USA" as your desired location, you may move in the right direction, but you won't know exactly where to go or when you've arrived.

If you enter from "Grand Central Station, New York" to "Santa Monica Pier, Santa Monica," you'll know the path, how to recognize if you're there, and how to track your progress. Growing should follow the exact same process, clearly specifying where you are today and your preferred destination. Most people slow their own growth because they aren't this clear about their development path.

Whether you use your company's individual development process or create a development plan on your own, you need to be precise and brutally honest with yourself about your origin and destination. This starts with a framework that my colleague Jim Shanley calls the "from/to," and it helps you understand exactly how you're perceived today and how you want to be seen in the future. The from/to is two brief statements—one describing where you are today and one describing your next big (not your ultimate) destination. Both statements should be direct, honest, and specific. When you read your from/to statements, you should be clear about which developmental step to take next.

Examples of great from/to statements include:

- From: An individual contributor who adds value through technical expertise and closely following others' directions.

- To: A people leader who creates a clear strategy and delivers results through a small team.

- From: A transformational marketing leader who relies on instinct to make decisions and relationships to get results.

- To: A complete CEO who embraces fact-based decision making and who displays the backbone to make tough, timely decisions.

- From: A business strategist who can appear aloof and dismissive of those with less intellectual horsepower.

- To: A general manager who aligns and inspires his region through personal connections and demonstrating genuine care for people.

Each is a clear, direct statement about where someone is and where they need to go. The directness of the from/to statements may surprise you, especially the third one. It's difficult but essential to be that clear about your own from/to if you want your development plan to be accurate. If those statements are vague, so are your start and finish coordinates. These from/to statements are real examples from successful executives who made tremendous progress once their needs were made this clear. Two are now CEOs—one of a $10 billion retail chain and another of a specialty eyewear company.

You'll get a precise from/to once you have input from others. The science is clear that everyone we work with sees us more accurately than we see ourselves, so it's their insights and opinions that should guide our journey. This is especially important if you consider yourself to be a high performer, because you're more likely to believe that your current skills and behaviors will maintain your success. That ignores the advice of Marshall Goldsmith, whose best-selling book reminds readers that "what got you here won't get you there."[8]

Your company's more senior leaders should guide your from/to because it's their opinions, not those of your peers or direct reports, that will decide how you progress in the organization. To get their direction:

- Identify who to ask. Choose your manager and two or three other senior leaders who you've worked with or who know your performance.

- Request their insights. Introduce the from/to concept to them, send them the from/to examples I gave earlier, and ask them to think about your from/to. Let them know it should only take a few minutes of their time, but that their thoughts will be tremendously helpful to you. Tell them to be brutally honest because their transparency will allow you to grow faster. You can meet with them to hear their insights or, if they're more transactional, allow them to respond by email. These leaders don't need to be experts in your function, although it helps if a few are. They just need to know you well enough to have an opinion of what's required for your future success in the organization.

- Develop your from/to statement. Use their input to create your final from/to. Which of their statements seem most direct and make you most uncomfortable? Which set the "to" far enough away so that it will be a meaningful challenge to achieve? Whose opinion do you trust the most? Use their statements as raw material and practice writing a few different from/to versions. Ask either the leaders who gave you the statements or some trusted colleagues for their thoughts on your draft versions. Develop your final from/to statement.

Now that your from/to statement clarifies your growth journey, focus on how to get there fast.

2. Get Experiences and Create Your Personal Experience Map

Since the 70/20/10 ratio indicates that experiences best accelerate your development, you should regularly ask yourself, "What next experience will most quickly move my career in the desired direction?" This question is helpful anytime in your career, from when you're flipping burgers to when you're a CEO. The key to being a high performer is to get as many successful, high-quality experiences as quickly as possible.

An experience is what you achieve when you deliver a high-quality outcome to a meaningful challenge. You may have to use many different skills and behaviors to deliver that outcome, but it's your ability to combine those together to deliver a result that creates an experience. For example, "create marketing strategy for a new line of business" is an experience. You may have to analyze the current market penetration and inspire a new team around a clear vision to get to that outcome. Those are tasks and behaviors, but they aren't an experience.

Experiences are your largest development tool, so you'll want to understand which will build your career and, more importantly, the few, most powerful experiences that can close your from/to gap. A regularly updated personal experience map should become your career guide.

A personal experience map shows which experiences you want to acquire in the next three to seven years to accelerate your career. It's a practical planning document that describes how you will produce the highest-performing you; "production" is the mindset you should have. Just as a manufacturer carefully plans how it will produce its products—what specifications it's building to, the manufacturing steps required, how it'll keep production moving—your experience map is your individual production plan. Each experience you have helps manufacture you into a more capable, confident, high performer.

Two types of experiences will accelerate your development—functional experiences and management experiences (see figure 3-3). Functional experiences help make you great at something—marketing, supply chain, R&D. They allow you to prove that you're highly competent at what you do. Management experiences help you to prove that you can perform or manage in a variety of challenging situations. You've not only been a great marketer in one region, but proven that you can lead marketing when you have a new team, in a turnaround situation and in a different geography. When you

FIGURE 3-3

Two types of experience

| Functional experiences | × | Management experiences | = | Faster growth |

You're great at something—finance, supply chain, general management, marketing.

You've delivered results under different management, leadership, and geographic challenges.

successfully achieve these challenging experiences, you prove to your company that you're a versatile leader who deserves a chance for larger, more important roles.

Now you can create your personal experience map by making the following moves.

INTERVIEW EXPERTS IN YOUR FIELD. What is ninetieth-percentile quality in your function or area? The best and brightest in your field can help you understand which experiences will get you into the top 10 percent and become an expert. Interview those leaders to learn which experiences will build your functional excellence. The interviews will give you the raw material to create your personal experience map.

- Identify the best experts. Ideally, you want to interview the best in your field, not the best in your company or country. If you want to be a chief financial officer (CFO), identify ten CFOs who you admire or who are well regarded in your industry. If your goal is to be great at early-stage pharma R&D, it's the same process. Find the leaders on industry "best" lists (best chief marketing officer, chief information officer, etc.) from their articles in trade magazines, on lists of speakers at relevant conferences, or from referrals of leaders in your company.

- Request an interview. Email each leader, framing your request as a casual conversation in which they can help someone in their field develop. You're asking them for their valuable time, so keep your request short and direct:

  - "Dear _____: Congratulations on being on the _____ list/I read your recent article in _____/Your colleague _____ referred me. As someone who's distinguished themselves in [your field], your insights would be very helpful as I continue my development. I know your time is valuable and I hope you can share fifteen to twenty minutes to tell me the four to five experiences you believe are most valuable to become a [position]. I am not looking for a job or internship from this conversation. Could we schedule a short call in the next few weeks?"

- Ask for insights. During your call, ask them the following question and take detailed notes:

  - "What are the key functional experiences [not necessarily jobs] that you believe will produce the highest-quality [general manager, IT architect, finance director]?" This question is only about making someone functionally great in [this field, function, discipline].

  - Another way to ask is, "Describe what you would see on the résumé of someone who is outstanding at _____ ." If you're having trouble getting quality information, ask them about the most valuable experiences they've had in their own careers.

  Thank them and ask permission to connect again if you have further questions. Offer to share your personal experience map with them. Interview a few different leaders, since their different perspectives will be valuable and their individual personal experiences will color their views. Also, expect that some people will easily answer your question, and others will struggle. They're smart executives, not development experts, so take their comments as a gift, even if some don't provide exactly the information you need.

CREATE YOUR PERSONAL EXPERIENCE MAP. Your interviews will provide you with raw material to create your personal experience map. Review your notes and list the experiences that your interviewees described. Not everything you heard will be useful; some information will overlap or contradict what another interviewee said. Your goal is to sort through this information to find the few experiences that will most accelerate your career.

An experience should describe a meaningful business outcome—open a new production facility, lead a large team through a business turnaround, or close books for a business unit. It should be a significant building block of your functional or leadership capability; your accomplishment of it should mean something to others in your field. Combine any experiences you've listed that are essentially the same and delete items that are behaviors or skills (see the differences in figure 3-4).

The functional experiences you need to be a high performer will be unique to your profession, but the management experiences will be very similar across professions. Management experiences grow generic capabilities that are valuable to all managers, no matter their function. For simplicity, use these experiences when you create your map (see figure 3-5).

FIGURE 3-4

Differences between experiences and behaviors or skills

Experiences	Behaviors	Skills
Drove car from home to work without having an accident.	Obeyed all traffic signals and was polite to other drivers.	Can operate a motor vehicle; able to read and understand road signs.
Built and opened a new widget factory in a developing country.	Understood and operated within the local culture; pushed team to meet aggressive deadlines.	Managed large-scale project, union relations, production scheduling for concrete.
Closed the books for a large business unit.	Quickly clarified discrepancies in ledgers; challenged leaders who suggested non-IFRS approach.	Has accounting, financial analysis, presentation, and reporting skills

FIGURE 3-5

Personal experience map

My goal position is _____ by _____

From: An individual contributor who adds value through technical expertise
and closely following directions

To: A people leader who creates a clear strategy and delivers results through
a small team following directions

Functional experiences I need	Management experiences I need
Planning experiences	**Life cycle experiences**
Lead large, complex cross-functional project or change initiative	Lead in a new market for our company
Develop a multiyear strategy and action plan	Lead the turnaround of a large facility or market
Plan, develop, and present "Holiday Initiative" to stakeholders	**Managing experiences**
	Manage in a matrix environment
Lead a significant cost-reduction initiative	Build a team from scratch
Sourcing experiences	Lead with more than four levels of organization reporting up to me
Lead a complex enterprise project	**Geographic experiences**
Manage enterprise engagement with a major supplier	Live and work in two countries outside of the United States and at least one where English is not the native language
Lead change in the area of sustainability by engaging internal/external stakeholders, including suppliers	
Lead a key supplier transition including managing risks, representing our company's values, and communicating to stakeholders	
Making experiences	
Manage a facility with 50+ people with a mix of professionals and shops-floor partners	

Likely barriers to my plan

-
-
-

How I will overcome barriers

-
-
-

- **Life-cycle experiences:** Lead in different parts of your company or product evolution. Lead in a turnaround situation, lead a startup, manage in a steady-state environment, work in a developing market or in a fully mature one.

- **Managing experiences:** Lead in environments where your managerial skills are tested. Upgrade a poor-quality team, lead a large team, manage a team where you have influence but not authority, lead in a matrixed environment, lead in a highly political environment.

- **Geographic experiences:** Have experiences outside your home geography where the local language is not your native language.

Select the four to seven functional experiences and three to four management experiences you believe will benefit you most and record them on your personal experience map. The map should be focused and realistic—a reference sheet that you'll use regularly to plan your growth and assess your progress.

The personal experience map is now your guide to continuously grow your high-performing self. Creating it will be one of your best investments of time. Review the content of your map any time you switch jobs or companies and at least every six months to ensure that it remains a current, helpful guide.

The personal experience map process is the one that my firm teaches to large, global companies to accelerate the growth of their talent, so I'm confident that it's a highly effective approach for you. You can use the template at www.the8steps.com to create your own map.

You now have control of your development because you know your from/to and have your personal experience map. There's one more thing to consider.

3. Get Feedback and Feedforward

Earlier we discussed the simple learning cycle of perform, feedback, and repeat. Your great experiences only matter if you treat them as learning opportunities from which you squeeze every ounce of feedback and insight. At the end of each experience, meet with the person who gave you the experience (this may or may not be your manager) for a structured debrief. Ask them:

- "In addition to delivering results, what did you hope I would learn from this experience? Do you believe I learned none, some, or all of that?"

- "Based on my performance, what advice would you have for me in similar types of experiences?"

- "Could you give me one other suggestion for how I can be a better performer going forward?"

WORK WITH YOUR COMPANY'S DEVELOPMENT PROCESS. Many companies have an annual process in which you and your manager plan your development. Your personal experience map should be your primary career guide and supplement your company's plan. To help ensure that you get what you need from your company's development process, do the following:

- Understand your manager's "one thing." You'd likely answer quickly if I asked you what one thing your spouse, child, parent, or best friend could do differently to be better in that role. Your boss has that same answer waiting for you—you just have to ask for it. Focus and clarity are powerful factors in development, so ask your manager, "What one thing can I change this year to be a higher performer than last year?" The answer should become your main goal in your company's individual development plan. You won't have time to complete two or three development activities, so focus on the one your manager believes is most powerful.

- **Lead with your personal experience map.** Your manager is not a development expert, and you shouldn't expect him or her to have perfect insights to your development. If you've prepared your personal experience map, lead the development conversation by saying, "I've thought about my goal to develop into a [position], and I think the next experience that would most accelerate my career development is _____." Listen to the response and, if she agrees, ask for a specific action to help you get that experience. If she disagrees but her suggestion is on your personal experience map, great! If it's not, use your influencing skills to convince her that you'll be a high performer in the experience you suggest. If that fails, decide if her development suggestion will keep your personal production process moving.

Sometimes managers' development suggestions will be a tactical step they would like to see you take, such as to attend a training course. In that case, agree to their suggestion, while also asking them to support the experience you seek as part of your experience map.

As you plan how to grow, keep these two hard truths in mind:

- **Your manager is not a development expert.** Managers are often tasked with creating their employees' development plans, so you might assume they are highly skilled in that area. Remember that your manager is not an expert in development. Their own career path may not be a model for yours, and they may not have accurate insights about the best way for you to advance. It's likely they've never been trained on how to create a great development plan. Given that, they should be one source of input, not the only source, for your personal development plan.

- Your company's formal development process may not be enough. You may not want to outsource your success to your employer but take personal responsibility for it instead. That mindset is helpful when considering your company's individual development process. My experience is that this process is typically not as rigorous as it should be. The development goals may be fuzzy. Your manager is typically not required to follow up on development plans. Participate in your company's process, but recognize that your real development plan should be the one you keep, update, and use to track your professional growth.

In short, high performers own their development and hold themselves accountable to achieve their goals.

Wrapping Up

You become a high performer with great results and the right behaviors. You remain a high performer by continually growing your capabilities and skills to position yourself for bigger, more challenging, and more career-building experiences. The surest way to grow yourself faster is to successfully complete as many of the right functional and management experiences as you can, as quickly as you can. Learn how to identify experiences from the best in the field and then own how you progress through them. You will always be your own best career advocate.

You now have strong results, great behaviors, and a plan to continuously improve. Step four, "connect," will show you how to build the strong internal and external networks that enable and sustain your success.

What Can Get in the Way

- My company wants me to take an assignment outside my home country, but I'm not sure it's the right thing to do. A move outside your home country will be one of the most powerful development experiences in your career. It will give you a fundamentally different perspective of the world and your home country culture, and how work gets done in different parts of the world. It's a key differentiator of success in many global companies, so unless it's impossible for you to move, you should take the assignment when offered. If you don't, you're limiting your ability to prove to others that you're a high performer.

- Shouldn't a development plan include behaviors and skills? Behaviors and skills matter tremendously, and in your experiences, you will gain new skills and practice new behaviors. If you want to develop a specific skill or behavior, determine which experiences will most effectively teach it to you.

- My company has a competency or behavior model that it says I should use for development. What is that and how do I connect these with experiences? A competency model can describe either behaviors your company wants you to demonstrate or capabilities it believes are important for your function. A behavioral competency might be "managing change," and the model will list that behavior and some examples. Competency models are helpful, but they don't tell you how to build the competencies. Experiences are the fastest way to build competencies, and if your manager insists on measuring or discussing competencies, ask him or her which experiences will help you most quickly build those competencies.

- If formal education is only 10 percent of learning, should I attend any courses that my company offers? Formal course work helps provide frameworks, tools, and the opportunity to discuss or practice concepts before implementing them. For those reasons alone, formal education can be very valuable. Be sure that you're not substituting a course for the learning that you could obtain through an experience.

- My company doesn't seem to prioritize experiences as a way to grow. That's fine. Guide your manager to help you get the experiences on your personal experience map. Review that map before any development conversation with your manager and prepare to ask for a specific experience(s). In that conversation, describe:

  - The benefits your manager or company will receive, that is, "I will be able to do x for you that I can't do now"; "I will be able to train others on this"; or "the company will get more of x or y from me."

  - How you plan to succeed in the experience (i.e., "I will use these skills, learn these new capabilities, demonstrate these behaviors, get this type of feedback to correct my course").

  Relieve their unspoken concern that you might leave their department or the company when you get these skills ("This experience will allow me to contribute to our team even more").

  If your manager turns you down multiple times when you request a new experience, ask them for very transparent feedback (i.e., "What one thing can I do that would best position me to get an experience like this in the future?"). They may think the experiences you're proposing are a significant stretch, and that your current performance isn't at a level where they're willing to invest in you or that your best learning will happen in your current role.

- I work in a small company, and I can't get much experience. Remember that experiences aren't jobs. They are opportunities to build your skills by delivering or doing something that you haven't delivered or done before. With that definition, are there other experiences that your company offers? There are always special projects. Will one of those help with an experience? Can you shadow someone in a function or who's doing a job that you'd like to know more about? If you can't find any experiences that will help your development, you need to decide if your company can help you to reach your career goals.

Remember and Apply

The research says:

- As working professionals, we grow our capabilities about 70 percent through our experiences, about 20 percent through others, and about 10 percent through formal learning.

- You'll get the most from experiences if they include challenges that are diverse (geographic, life cycle, management) and adverse (you must solve new problems to succeed in them).

You should:

- Create your personal experience map by asking experts in your field to identify the most meaningful experiences to gain.

- Write and maintain your individual development plan—your lifetime guide for how you will achieve high performance.

- Regularly evaluate if you're having the most powerful learning experience you can; change quickly if not.

Try using:

- Personal experience map (figure 3-5)

Step 4

Connect

P resident Lyndon Johnson acquired and used power in ways many would consider blatantly manipulative. A master of influence, he was elected as a US senator at age forty (the average age for senators at the time was fifty-eight) and as the youngest-ever Senate majority leader at age forty-five.[1] Historian Robert A. Caro, who won two Pulitzer Prizes for his books about Johnson, describes Johnson's deliberate approach to building his connections:

> Johnson was brilliant in the way he went about choosing mentors. He was very deliberate about it. After he was elected to the Senate—before he was even sworn in—he sought out Bobby Baker, a 21-year-old cloakroom clerk, because he had heard that Baker knew "where the bodies were buried." And what did he want to ask Baker? Not what the Senate rules were but who had the power. Bobby Baker told Johnson that there was only one man in the Senate who had the power— Richard Russell. This was perhaps the single most important piece of information that Lyndon Johnson acquired during his first year in office. And what was Johnson's first act in the Senate? It wasn't to rise on the floor and speak. It wasn't to sponsor legislation. It was to get close to Richard Russell. Most senators—maybe all senators but Lyndon Johnson— come to the Senate and look for the most powerful, the most prestigious committee to get on. That's not what Johnson did.

Once he knew that Russell was the power in the Senate, he checked to see what Russell's committee was. It was Armed Services. So, Lyndon Johnson asked to be on the Armed Services committee. And because nobody else wanted to be on that committee, he got straight in . . .

He worked on Russell's vulnerabilities. Russell was lonely. He had no life outside the Senate. He would come to the Capitol every Saturday because he had no place else to go. So, Johnson went to the Capitol every Saturday. Russell ate at little diners around the Capitol, and Johnson began to accompany him to a few hamburger joints after work. Soon they're eating together nearly every day. Russell loved baseball, but he had no one to go to games with. Johnson had no interest in baseball whatsoever, but he told Russell he loved it and went to games with him. And, as with all these older men, he flattered him outrageously. Russell was proud of his legislative artistry; Johnson nicknamed him "the Old Master." When Russell would give him a piece of advice, Johnson would say, "Well, that's a lesson from the Old Master. I'll remember that."[2]

Why It Matters

Johnson mastered the art of connecting, even if he likely didn't know the powerful science behind its benefits. That science shows that influencing and connecting strategies are amazingly effective to get what you need from superiors and peers. Your ability to get these additional resources and relationships is essential to reaching your theoretical maximum performance. Better yet, your ability to connect is almost entirely controllable by you.

Despite its scientifically proven benefits, you may be somewhat squeamish, embarrassed, or skeptical to use the strategies I will describe. You're not alone. One research article said that many "people struggle first and foremost with the idea of networking as futile, threatening or morally questionable."[3] Fortunately, networking is not futile, because it's proven to work. It may feel threatening at first, but like all challenging things, you will become more comfortable each time you do it. You'll need to decide if strategically connecting with others fits within your moral framework.

If you're not fully convinced about using the strategies I describe in this chapter, consider the words of Stanford Graduate School of Business professor Jeffrey Pfeffer, who teaches the school's highly popular course on the topic of power. Pfeffer says, "I am increasingly convinced that people who have power are not necessarily smarter than others. Beyond a certain level of intelligence and level in the hierarchy, everyone is smart. What differentiates people is their political skill and savvy . . . those who have power a) understand that the world is not always a just and fair place and accept that fact, b) understand the bases and strategies for acquiring power, and c) take actions consistent with their knowledge in a skillful way."[4]

Pfeffer is clear (and the science supports) that strategies that help you connect with others will benefit your career. Like each of the eight steps, you can choose whether to take it or not, but I'd suggest that you're consciously suboptimizing your performance if you don't. That's why "connect" is step four to high performance.

The extensive research about the benefits of building great relationships says:

- Ingratiate yourself and everything works better. If you ingratiate yourself with others, you will benefit in every typical work scenario—better performance reviews, more successful interviews, stronger peer relationships, and so on. This may not be your preferred approach, but it works when used. The opposite strategy of aggressively stating your point of view with others has been tested as well. The result? It typically backfires.[5]

- Relationships can supplement weak performance. Poorly performing employees who have strong relationships with their managers get higher performance ratings despite their objectively low performance. There's no stronger proof for the benefits of connecting well with your boss than the fact that obvious low performance can be missed or ignored because of a strong relationship.[6]

- You move as fast as your boss does. Your positive relationship with your manager improves your promotion chances, and employees get promoted faster when their manager gets promoted faster.[7]

- Big network, big results. Those with stronger networks have higher salaries, more promotions over their careers, and greater career satisfaction. It's not just who you know, but how many you know as well.[8] Those who connect more effectively have higher performance because they're able to get more insights, favors, and answers from more people.[9]

Science tells us that your personality and political skills directly affect your ability to connect and influence, including:

- The context predicts who connects best. Both introverts and extroverts can connect effectively, but who they connect with will depend on the context. Introverts are more influential in technical settings where their primary focus is to work on tasks. Extroverts are more influential in team-based environments where their natural interest in connecting gives them an advantage.[10]

- Connectors are far more positive. Those who connect well have higher self-confidence, job satisfaction, belief in the organization, commitment, productivity, positive behaviors, career success, and personal reputation.[11] The research isn't clear about which influences which.

- Political animals have an advantage. Your ability to master good politics makes you more effective because political environments make many people unhappy, less committed, more stressed, and wanting to leave the organization.[12] Those who can master a more political environment have a distinct performance advantage over those who can't.

- Your peers will keep you in check. Ingratiation works well with your boss, but remember that your peers will see you play that game. If they think you're trying too hard or too obviously to build that connection, it can harm your reputation and network. The more you might benefit from the relationship with your manager, the more risk your behaviors pose to your reputation and relationships with your peers.[13]

What to Do

You should develop and actively implement a strategy to connect better with your manager, peers, and subordinates, and with your external network. Each connection provides unique benefits but requires a different strategy to succeed.

Connect with Your Manager

Your immediate manager is your most critical work relationship. The science is clear that the strength of that relationship strongly influences your success. Your priority connection activity should be to build a close, productive relationship with him or her. The tactics that will get you there are quite straightforward.

PERFORM. If you consistently deliver great results, you build the foundation for a great relationship with your boss. Your high performance makes her look good and reduces the effort she needs to spend managing you, so it's a double win for her. Although science says that if you're great at ingratiating yourself with your boss, your actual performance matters less, that's a rather risky long-term strategy. At some point, you'll have a new boss who will value your sucking up only *in addition to* your performance, not in place of it.

HELP DELIVER WHAT MATTERS. Your boss wants to look good to those above and around her. A surefire connecting strategy is to know what will make her look good and help her achieve that. The easiest way to determine this is to ask, "What's on your agenda right now?" or "What's the one deliverable, project, or metric that you really want to ace this year or quarter?"

Once you know her concerns, identify and offer specific ways you can help. Don't just ask, "Is there anything I can do to help?" Give options for how you can support her. If she has a big presentation coming up, offer to help with the research, gather data, assemble the presentation, or review it. If there's an upcoming sales meeting, volunteer to conduct research on the company, on its products, or on the target company's executive team.

Put conscious effort into asking your boss that question and following up afterward. You will possibly be the only one who does this, which makes this approach even more effective. Even if your manager says no the first time, ask regularly. You'll get credit for your positive intentions.

FLATTER. No matter how humble we think we are, it's amazing how much we like to hear others praise our capabilities and accomplishments. Flattery can be "great presentation" or "you seem to really know what's going on around here." People love to be complimented and think more positively about those who compliment them.[14] While it's theoretically possible to go overboard, science says that even when people know we're false in our flattery, they'll still feel good about it and us.[15] Your boss is human—she has the same insecurities that you do. You'll gain significant goodwill if you regularly make her feel good about herself and her value at work.

OFFER GENUINE PERSONAL FRIENDSHIP. The most obvious way to build a strong relationship is to become your boss's friend. That positive relationship will have great benefits that last longer than those you'll get through more transactional connecting strategies. You build that friendship as you would any other, through regular contacts, trusting actions, listening, and acting selfless.

Pay attention to your boss's personal interests as well. You don't have to become an expert in offshore powerboat racing, cricket, quilting, or whatever unique hobby she has, but if she conspicuously mentions or displays something that indicates an interest, occasionally ask about it. Don't fake expertise in her favorite interest. You'll lose huge amounts of goodwill if you say you love Formula One auto racing but can't name your favorite driver, team, or track.

While anyone can apply any of these tactics, women engage in impression management less often than men. Whether it's self-promotion, sucking up, or aggressively stating your case, men are more likely to actively try to connect and persuade people they work with.[16] Some of these tactics are incredibly effective to improve the quality and depth of important relationships. When women don't use these tactics to advance their careers, they're limiting their success. These are behaviors—completely controllable and learnable—that women should use to better position themselves to be high performers.

Connect with Your Peers

Peers play a unique role in your quest to be a high performer because they have no direct power over your success but significant influence. Strong connections with them help ensure that they don't hold you back, even if they have less ability to move you forward. Four things will help you connect.

KNOW THEM WELL. You'll understand how to best connect with your peers when you know them well. Whether you work in a large or small organization; in Europe, Asia, or North America; all in one building or spread across the globe, you need to actively execute a plan to get to know every key peer personally. You should call or have lunch, beer, coffee, or any other meaningful connection with every key peer at least once a quarter. This is more than saying "hi" for a moment in the lunchroom. This is a scheduled, "Hey, I'd love to catch up," sit-down meeting with the goal of understanding what's going on with them at work and perhaps at home. You don't have to like everyone equally, but you can't understand how to best work with your peers until you know them well.

CONNECT MORE WITH THE BEST. Your reputation depends on your relationships with many peers, but your future is more influenced by your relationships with your high-performing peers. Those high performers may be competing for the same promotion or resources as you. That makes it important to show that you don't have the proverbial knife behind your back and that you'll be either a good boss or a direct report, depending on who gets promoted.

Your boss also likely trusts your highest-performing peers, so when they talk to him about you, their comments will matter more than comments from a low-performing peer. Finally, you're known by the company you keep, so would you rather be seen as a compatriot of the best talent or of average talent?

SAY YES. There's a powerful psychological concept called the norm of reciprocity. In short, it says that we're hardwired to want to help someone if they help us.[17] Use this to your benefit by saying yes when your peers request help, especially your high-performing peers. This may include lending them a resource to directly support a project or even throwing a few budget dollars to them when they're in need. This type of selfless behavior builds your image and gives you credit with the person you've done it for.

ASK FOR HELP AND ADVICE. People are flattered when you ask for their opinions. Even if you have a perfectly thought-out strategy, plan, or document, ask some key peers for input. This works especially well if there's something in your plans that might conflict with theirs or you're working in an area where they are also an expert. It makes them feel smart, makes you appear humble, and you may even get some valuable insights along the way.

Connect with Your Subordinates

In step two, "behave to perform," I showed how connecting with your direct reports is a key part of being a transformational leader. The unique factor about connecting with your direct reports is that you already have power and organizational authority over them, so it's helpful to manage these relationships, but it's not as essential as managing the relationships with your manager or peers.

Build Your External Network

You will be a higher performer when you build strong networks inside and outside your organization. That strong network gives you more access to valuable information (what's happening in the industry; who's important to know), more resources (more proverbial neighbors to borrow a cup of sugar from), and more people who can actively sponsor and support your career.[18]

The fixed 50 percent can help or hinder you when building your network, because extroverts more naturally, easily, and frequently form relationships of every kind.[19] But since the size and strength of your network will help your performance, even introverts need to engage in (or fake) those network-building behaviors.

In step two, you learned that some behaviors will help you become known and others will help sustain your success over time. The same is true for your networks. A smaller, tighter network that's more related to your position at work (i.e., your IT or finance peers) helps you to develop credibility within your organization. That internal network is essential to your success at work but, because it's insular, it's not likely to improve your image in the profession, increase how many executive recruiters know you, or accelerate your career advancement.

Your broad networks extend your reach to people who can advance your career, connect you with important contacts, and informally coach you to success. You can build those networks through personal connections made at events, conferences, professional association gatherings, coffees, lunches, and dinners.[20]

Extroverts may just need a great plan to develop their network; introverts need a plan and something that compels them to overcome their fears of connecting. For introverts like me, there are a few thoughts to keep in mind:

- Everyone loves to talk about themselves. You don't need to worry if you can't engage in an hour of witty discussion filled with fascinating stories about your unique interests. People are naturally egocentric and often happy to share those details about themselves instead. Your job is to memorize five questions that will keep any conversation going (where are they from originally, where did they work before their current employer, vacation plans for this year, what they like to do outside of work, etc.).

- People want to help you (if it's easy or in their self-interest). People connect partly for the political benefits, and an essential part of politics is to return favors (remember the norm of reciprocity). If you wonder why anyone would want to network with you, they may see you as someone who can help them today or tomorrow, they may be building their own network, they may just be nice people, or they may actively want to help others succeed. You should use that powerful psychology to your benefit.

  Make the connection easy for them. Go to their office or a coffee shop near them, schedule the meeting for no more than thirty minutes, and request nothing from them except to stay in touch in the future.

- They notice you less than you think (and that's good). There's a concern that makes us self-conscious and less will-ing to put ourselves in networking situations. The spotlight effect is a psychological phenomenon in which we believe that others notice our actions and appearance far more than they actually do. If you're nervous that you might say or do something embarrassing in a long conversation with a new colleague or networking contact, realize that others don't notice unique things about us nearly as much as we think.[21]

And, if you do something silly like forget a critical name in a conversation, research tells us that people don't harshly judge mistakes that they can imagine making themselves.[22]

- Extroverts have more relationships, but not more meaningful relationships. Extroverts' social networks are larger, but they don't have any deeper connections with their contacts than introverts do.[23]

There are many networking tactics you can apply, but I recommend you start your efforts with a strong foundation and strategy for building your connections.

HAVE A PURPOSE AND BE PURPOSEFUL. You'll find it much easier to create your networking plan once you're clear on your purpose for networking. Are you trying to learn more about your function or industry? Are you trying to become better known so you can be more influential? Are you trying to find a new job? Your answer will guide how broad or focused your contact base should be, the level of individuals you should network with, how you structure the conversation with them, and much more.

Once you're clear on your purpose, develop your plan. How many contacts do you need to make? Over what period of time? In what industries or locations? How many real connections (meetings and calls, not LinkedIn contacts) will you make every month? How will you evaluate your success? Connecting only delivers powerful benefits if you do it. If you want to be a successful networker, you need to manage and monitor your progress the same way you would any other important project.

BE STRATEGIC—NOT ALL CONTACTS ARE EQUAL. You want to meet with the most powerful, highest-ranking, prominent, well-respected contacts that you can. In your casual networking, it's fine to meet the supply chain director from the local factory. He's a nice guy, and someone you'll be able to chat with at future events. If your purpose is to accelerate your career growth, the most powerful individuals will have the most influence. Fortunately, the exact same ingratiation strategies that you use on your boss work equally well with other powerful individuals.

Invite them for coffee, lunch, or dinner with a clearly stated purpose—to better understand the industry, learn from their career experiences, and so on. Say nice things about their accomplishments. Express interest in their interests. They will often be happy to share their stories and even introduce you to other powerful people because they often know other powerful people.

BECOME THE NETWORK. When I was a corporate executive, I was frustrated when organizations approached me for paid networking and said, "Pay us $10,000 and you can hang out with others in your field four times a year." I thought that I could call ten people in my field instead and set up a great discussion without paying anyone anything. I started the New Talent Management Network with that goal in mind—help those in my profession learn and network. It's now the largest network of its kind, is 100 percent free, offers meetings in cities across the United States, and conducts meaningful research in the field. There was no network I believed in, so I started my own. If there's no network that meets your needs, start one. There's no better way to network than to become the network.

USE EXTERNAL CONSULTANTS AS CONNECTORS. In any field, there are external consultants who will regularly knock on your door to sell you a product or service. You likely ignore most of them. Start thinking of those consultants as people who can help you connect. They see hundreds of people a year in your function or industry. Tell the consultants that you'll meet with them in exchange for networking introductions to three high-quality contacts.

Build Your Assessment

Now that you know the types of connections to make and how, you need to plan and track your connection strategy. You'll build stronger connections the same way you achieve any other goal, with focus and discipline. The connection planning sheet can help you track your key relationships and regularly plan how to strengthen them (see figure 4-1 for a sample). Fill in the chart with the names of your key connections, your last connection with them, your next planned connection, and any notes that will help you to customize your interactions. This planned approach to connecting will ensure that extroverts focus on the few connections that matter most and introverts regularly connect, even when it's not their natural focus.

Wrapping Up

Connecting can be one of the most challenging elements of becoming a high performer because you can't directly control its success, there are social conventions you must follow, and some people are naturally more comfortable with it than others. The great news is that your network will multiply your success. A strong network will bring you the contacts, insights, and resources that will help you be a high performer. The science is clear that building great relationships, even by ingratiating yourself with others, will advance your career.

FIGURE 4-1

Connection planning sheet—2019

Internal	Relationship strength	Last formal connection	Next formal connection	Key considerations/Notes
Boss	Medium	Jan. 2019 Lunch	Apr. 2019 Lunch	Big goal for the year is successful opening of new Mexico City factory; concerned about union issue; daughter Suzie leaving for university in Aug.
Other senior leader	High	Mar. 2019 Presented project report	Nothing scheduled	Looking for legacy; develop short list of ideas that would give him high visibility and allow positive, high visibility 2020 exit.
Peer 1	Low	Nov. 2018 Coffee at exec. retreat	Apr. 2019 Lunch	Preoccupied with systems launch; heard that she doesn't think I can be of help; go to Apr. lunch with three ideas for how I and my team can support her; let her know all in the background and at her direction.
Peer 2	High	Feb. 2019 Sideline of kid's soccer game	June 2019 Present together at conference	All good. Make sure to ask her about balance of time she wants for conference presentation. Offer her technical section where she can "shine."
Peer 3	Medium	Mar. 2019 Monthly touch-base meeting	Apr. 2019 Monthly touch-base meeting	Relationship at operational level; no immediate opportunity to improve quality. Give his team member Juan an opportunity to run Project Social to gain N.A. visibility.
Peer 4	Medium	Dec. 2018 Lunch	Apr. 2019 Starting monthly touch-base mtg.	Increase frequency of meetings given her likely move to EMEA Marketing. Make sure she gets to know Madison to position her for #2 role.
Peer 5	High	Jan. 2019 Drinks at Hoolihans	Apr. 2019 Starting monthly touch-base mtg.	Contacts are good but too infrequent; monthly meetings will help me better understand his 2019 agenda.
Peer 6	Medium	Mar. 2019 Coffee	Apr. 2019 Coffee	He shares more when we leave the office, so continue monthly coffees. Ask if he's concerned about the Corn Crunchers product launch. Hinted at that last time. If so, see if he's connected with Chicago Consulting Company.

(continued)

FIGURE 4-1 (Continued)

External	Relationship strength	Last formal connection	Next formal connection	Key considerations/Notes
Contact 1	Medium	Mar. 2019 Call	Send article on social media strategies	Mentioned lack of social media strategy past two connections. Introduce him to Chloe for an informal conversation.
Contact 2	Low	Dec. 2018 Email; no response	Call and offer coffee/lunch when in Atlanta	Heard that he went tuna fishing with Max in Gulf in January. Mention in next conversation and tell him about Goldsmith fishing charters in San Diego.
Contact 3	High	Jan. 2019 Office visit in L.A.	May 2019 She will visit when in Paris	Send restaurant recommendations for Paris.
Contact 4	Medium	Jan. 2019 Office visit in Singapore	Apr. 2019 Check-in call	Find out the types of connections that would be most helpful for her. Introduce her to two people by June.

You now have a strong foundation for continued high performance with great goals, the right behaviors, a plan to grow, and a network to support you. There are a few more actions you should consider to extract the most power from steps one through four. When you understand how your company's needs will change, you can adapt your behaviors and mindset to keep your performance high in nearly every business challenge. Step five, "maximize your fit," gives you the tips and tools to do exactly that.

What Can Get in the Way

- **I believe in building genuine relationships. This approach sounds fake.** A network relationship is a genuine relationship if you're honest with others about why you're building it. If you tell someone you're connecting to "get to know other people in our industry" or "keep up with the current trends in our function," it doesn't matter if you later use those insights or connections to find a better job or sell more products. The person you connected with assumed you would put that knowledge to use and would likely be disappointed if the time they spent with you was never beneficial.

- **I feel uncomfortable asking someone a level above me in my company to coffee or lunch.** Unless your country or company culture is one that would discourage that behavior, you need to actively build relationships with people at the level above you. They will make decisions about your career, and the better they know you, the more positive those decisions are likely to be. If you're uncertain how to make the invitation, let them know you'd like to learn more about their position and what they do. You can also ask someone who knows them well if they'd typically accept that type of invitation. Even if only two of the five people you invite say yes, you've made two new connections that can help you be a high performer.

- I can't spend that much time connecting. Who should I prioritize? You should build strong relationships with your manager and your two or three highest-performing peers. Outside your company, connect with the most influential person in your field. You may need to invite ten external contacts before one responds to your note, but you'll benefit from the insights and connections of any strong influencer in your field.

- Shouldn't I spend more time connecting with my direct reports? You'll naturally interact with your direct reports as their manager, but you might not naturally spend time with your peers or boss. If your direct reports are already engaged and productive, investing too much more in those relationships can take away from your limited time to build additional connections sideways and upward.

Remember and Apply

The science says:

- Extroverts are more natural connectors but don't have higher-quality networks than introverts.

- Those with larger networks have higher salaries, more promotions, and greater satisfaction during their careers.

- People are most interested in connecting when there are obvious benefits for them, but typically will positively respond to your request due to the norm of reciprocity.

You should:

- Establish a strong relationship with your boss that's based both on your excellent performance and on an active strategy to help them perform well and look great to others.

- Identify your highest-performing peers and build a strong relationship with each by understanding their needs, helping them where possible, and engaging in social behavior like having coffee or lunch with them.

- Identify the most influential people in your field and build relationships with a few of them by showing that you're a loyal follower and want to help them be even more successful.

Try using:

- Connection planning sheet (figure 4-1)

Step 5

Maximize Your Fit

M ore than one-third of the companies you know today won't exist in twenty-five years. The speed of the corporate life cycle—birth, growth, success, and failure— has accelerated so quickly that it's predicted the average company today will exist for less than eleven years.[1] As those companies rapidly change, what they need from their leaders and employees changes too. That means the capabilities that made you successful in one part of the company's life cycle may be less valuable when the company changes.

Are you great at helping the company grow? Fine, but we're in a turnaround mode, so what can you do for us now? Do you pride yourself on being a change leader? Thank you, but we're done with transformation and don't need you to unnecessarily shake things up. Companies change faster than people change. You'll only stay a high performer if you adapt your capabilities and approach to what your company needs at that moment. Two Coca-Cola CEOs learned that lesson the hard way.

Fit, Failure, and Recovery at Coke

Coca-Cola's board of directors understood the massive changes facing their industry in 1997 when they selected their CFO Doug Ivester to replace Coke's legendary, but terminally ill, CEO Bob Goizueta. Coke had dominated the beverage market for decades, but the emergence of bottled waters, energy drinks, and alternative beverages now threatened its leadership position. Coke had to respond to these threats with innovative products and an organization that could quickly and nimbly navigate this new landscape. Goizueta had effectively set that strategy in motion.

Ivester was an eighteen-year Coke veteran widely viewed as a brilliant, controlling leader who became the iconic company's CFO at age thirty-seven. An accountant by training, he had a masterful control of details and deep pride in his financial acumen, once bragging that "I know how all the levers work and I could generate so much cash I could make everybody's head spin." Those capabilities allowed Ivester to deliver outstanding results as a CFO, but were they the right raw material for Coke's next CEO?[2]

In promoting Ivester, Coke's board of directors assumed that being smart, hard-driving, and detail-oriented were skills that would benefit their future CEO. Those are wonderful capabilities, but Coke's strategy during the 1990s cola wars demanded innovation and rapid change. Science suggests that leaders who deliver innovation and rapid change are those who personally connect with subordinates, communicate a clear direction, and give broad autonomy to their team members.[3] These were not Ivester's strengths—he was known as a controlling, structured, and reserved leader.[4]

The misfit between Coke's needs and Ivester's capabilities showed up quickly and painfully. In the two years after his appointment as CEO, Coke's earnings declined and its market value, which had been steadily rising for sixteen years, went flat. Ivester appeared to have a tin ear with bottlers, partners, and employees.[5] Shortly after his two-year anniversary as CEO, the Coke board let Ivester go.

The board selected longtime Coke executive Doug Daft to replace Ivester as CEO. Daft had led parts of Coca-Cola's Asia Pacific region and was known as a consensus builder and diplomat, but not as a strong communicator. Some at Coke considered him to be an indecisive leader. Coke's strategy still demanded innovation and change, but Daft's fit with those needs appeared to be no better than Ivester's. Shortly after starting as CEO, he announced a large restructuring to reduce costs and head counts at Coke's Atlanta headquarters. That move suggested he was less focused on the growth and innovation strategy and more on creating an efficient organization. Under Daft's leadership, Coke reported years of lackluster results that drove the stock price lower and weakened its ability to compete with Pepsi. He announced his retirement just four years after taking the job.

Coke's board then began its search for the company's fourth CEO in just seven years—an endeavor that became a highly watched and highly embarrassing spectacle. Over the next months, it was publicly reported which CEOs were offered Coke's CEO job; all had refused it. Eventually, the board hired a retired Coke executive, Neville Isdell, as CEO.

Isdell's words and actions quickly showed that he fit well with Coke's innovation and change strategy. He rejected the premise that Coke should compete on price, started to reinvest in people, and spoke often and directly about the desired direction of the company. With Isdell being an apparently good fit with Coke's strategy, the company's stock price and market share against Pepsi quickly recovered. But, seven years of leadership that did not fit the strategy had cost Coke, and its two departed CEOs, dearly.

Why It Matters

The lesson from Coke's CEO tribulations is about fit, not failure. Each of its CEOs was very smart, highly capable, and accomplished, but no one excels at everything. When their capabilities aligned with the organization's needs (i.e., Ivester being brilliant at finance), they produced wonderful results. When there were gaps in the fit, it was disastrous.

If your personal capabilities and interests match what your company needs, you're better positioned to succeed. It's this fit, not just individual brilliance, that science says helps predict strong performance. Unfortunately, stories about high-performing leaders often focus on the singular qualities they bring to the table—intellectual horsepower, blinding charisma, industry expertise. But there are two parts to performance—what you're able to deliver and what your company needs you to deliver. High performance is far more likely if you can master the fit between those two parts.

Fit matters because companies change as they respond to their markets and customers, as their products mature, or as they find new business opportunities. Those changes may mean a shift in how they manage the business and in the culture that will grow the company. When those fundamental elements of the company change, what the company needs from its talent often changes as well.

While the company may have once valued that brash, brilliant sales leader who always achieves results, his "get it done any way you can" approach to performance now undermines the company's goals for more disciplined and efficient execution. That long-tenured manager who quietly executes, is highly introverted, and risk averse? She will have trouble executing the bold change demanded by the private equity firm that just purchased her company. If you think your strengths will always be strengths, think again. Since companies change faster than people change, great performers can become average performers overnight when their company changes the definition of "great."

High performers continually adjust and maximize their fit with their company. They know that their ability to quickly shift their behaviors to align with new strategies and changed needs makes them more versatile, valuable, and more likely to get opportunities to demonstrate even more high performance. Step five for high performance is to "maximize your fit."

What We Know

Science tells us that people who fit with an organization deliver better results because they're more satisfied with their jobs and more committed to the company.[6] It's a rather intuitive and very powerful scientific concept called, not surprisingly, person-organization fit.[7] But how do you fit with a company?

Science suggests that two key ways people fit are with a company's strategy and with the amount of change the company needs.[8] "Strategy" describes how your company plans to beat the competition. "Change" describes the level of turmoil you'll need to manage as it does that. Your fit with strategy and change will help predict if you'll be a high performer. These two elements also evolve regularly at your company, and its evolution is why actively managing your fit is necessary.

Companies change quickly. Executives regularly update their company's strategy to respond to fluctuating market conditions, regulatory changes, products' movement through their life cycle, and many other factors. Within twelve months, a company may move from a growth mode to a turnaround mode or from trying to develop cutting-edge products to focusing on being a low-cost provider. The company can quickly wrench its processes and practices to support those changes, but it's far more challenging for employees to shift their behaviors and capabilities at the same speed.

People change slowly. Our fixed 50 percent won't meaningfully change, and even parts of the flexible 50 percent can work against our ability to change. If you've tried hard for ten years to perform, behave, and grow in a way that supports your company's steady-as-she-goes, low-cost strategy, you've likely built strong capabilities in that area. You've had ten years of practice and ten years of aligning your mindset to achieve that goal. Now, your company has asked you to innovate and do it quickly. That's a pivotal moment for any employee and one that can separate those who will remain high performers from those who will slip. The first step to maximize your fit is to recognize what you and your company contribute to fit.

WHAT YOU CONTRIBUTE TO FIT.   You have a preferred way of working and preferred type of company to work in. You might love the fast-paced, frenetic, risky environment of a small, high-growth firm. You might enjoy the stability, professionalism, and predictable environment of a well-established, larger firm. You likely have a preference between those choices, but you can adapt to a *somewhat* different environment if needed. However, since your fixed 50 percent has a strong influence on your core preferences, you'll have to work harder to maintain your fit if your work environment doesn't align with the one that you naturally prefer.

WHAT YOUR COMPANY CONTRIBUTES TO FIT.   Your company has a culture, a strategy, and a preference for how it gets work done. Those factors create the environment that you must fit within. Yet these factors may change quickly. Competitive pressures, innovation, and even a company's natural evolution mean that the company you joined just a few years ago may have very different talent needs today.[9]

That pace of change means that you have to change when the company decides its strategy requires new behaviors or capabilities. If you don't actively manage your fit as your company's needs change, you will find it more difficult to be a high performer, no matter how hard you try to master the other seven steps.

What to Do

If you regularly assess your company's changing needs, you can shift your capabilities and behaviors to better align with them. That assessment requires you to:

- Understand your company's changing needs.

- Understand where you naturally fit.

- Manage your fit to maximize your performance.

Understand Your Company's Changing Needs

As your company's strategy and change needs evolve, the capabilities that define high performance will evolve as well. The more accurately you understand these changes, the faster you'll be able to align your behaviors with the new definition of high performance.

WHAT IS YOUR COMPANY'S STRATEGY? An organization's strategy typically focuses on achieving one of two goals—win by being the most innovative company or win by being the most efficient company. Each strategy requires different capabilities and mindsets in order to succeed. Winning through innovation may require greater risk taking, creativity, and comfort with ambiguity. Winning through efficiency may take more dispassionate thinking, a process orientation, and Six Sigma capabilities. You may argue that a company must do both to succeed. While both are important, science says that a pure strategy (trying to win by being the most efficient *or* the most innovative) will always outperform a blended strategy of trying to be kind of good at each.[10]

WHAT ARE YOUR COMPANY'S CHANGE NEEDS? An organization may be going through a merger, economic shock, rapid growth, turnaround, or similar event that demands leaders who can manage major changes. Or, it may just be experiencing the typical ups and downs that mark daily life in most organizations. Your success in each scenario requires very different capabilities.

You may know leaders who thrive when there's chaos and churn around them. They have a unique ability to take smart risks, craft a concise vision, and relentlessly drive progress—they're more transformational.[11] Other leaders are tremendously effective managing the day-to-day challenges of the business. They execute core processes, manage their team well, and are good corporate citizens in typical times. But that day-to-day leader will be in far over his head if asked to lead massive change, and that leader who thrives in turmoil will be bored senseless in a calmer environment.

If you combine the strategy and the change concepts, you end up with a four-box grid I call the fit matrix that you can use to assess how you fit with different company environments (see figure 5-1).

FIGURE 5-1

The fit matrix

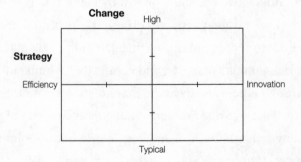

Understand Where You Naturally Fit

Since you know that fit matters, you should develop in the right direction to maximize fit and performance. That starts by identifying where you naturally fit. How you fit is driven by your personality (fixed 50 percent), the capabilities you've gained during your career, and the work environment you prefer. Those combined factors cause you to prefer a certain way of working and make you more capable in some situations than in others. In this way, you're like a puzzle piece. You have a distinct shape that may be interesting on its own, but that's even more valuable when it fits with the other pieces.

For example, Amazon's founder and CEO Jeff Bezos is a brilliantly innovative leader who's led Amazon through multiple waves of innovation—from an online bookstore to e-tailing platforms to products (Kindle, Fire) to services (Amazon Web Services) to new industries (Whole Foods). He's built a highly efficient company along the way, but Amazon wins in the market because it is innovative.

Now take Bezos—one of the most successful corporate leaders in history—and make him CEO of Exxon Mobil, where he would have to lead an efficiency-focused company. Would he be the best CEO for that job? Fit suggests he would be a fine CEO but not necessarily the best choice. His personality, preferences, and years of practice have made him a great fit for a specific type of challenge, and sucking oil out of the ground isn't it. The fact that he's incredibly smart and capable doesn't mean that he's the most capable leader in every possible situation. His puzzle piece fits with some, but not all, puzzles.

Let's assess where you naturally fit best in the fit matrix.

FIRST, DETERMINE YOUR NATURAL FIT. Follow the instructions in the fit matrix assessment to quickly assess yourself and understand your preferred fit with a company.

Fit Matrix™ Assessment

SECTION 1: Fit with strategy

The statements below describe different types of work environments. Please read the two statements on each line. Mark the box that more closely describes the work environment or challenges that most interest you. If neither phrase perfectly describes your interests, please mark the item that most closely matches your preference.

	Column A		Column B	
	Do you prefer this?		Or do you prefer this?	
1	Expand to new markets and develop new customers	☐	Streamline existing processes and find efficiencies	☐
2	A role with high risk and the potential for large rewards	☐	A role with moderate risk and the potential for moderate rewards	☐
3	Grow a new business	☐	Turn around a failing business	☐
4	Find profits by developing new products or services	☐	Find profits by improving existing practices	☐
5	Make decisions quickly but without some critical data	☐	Make decisions slowly but with all relevant data	☐
6	Sell new ideas	☐	Perfect existing ideas	☐
7	A role requiring moderate attention to detail	☐	A role requiring strong attention to detail	☐
8	A role focused on ideas and possibilities	☐	A role focused on execution and practical considerations	☐
9	A role where you do not have to monitor task progress	☐	A role where you actively monitor task progress	☐
10	Create a new work process		Improve an existing work process	☐
	Total		Total	
	A. Divided by 2 =		B. Divided by 2 =	

SECTION 1 ANSWER: Subtract column B from column A (A minus B) =

1. Count the number of marks in each column.

2. Divide each number by 2.

3. Subtract the result in column B from the result in column A. Write down that number. It may be negative.

SECTION 2: Fit with change

Which phrase best matches how people who know you well would describe you? Check one box for each row.

	Column A		Column B	
	Would those who know you well describe you like this?		**Or like this?**	
1	More dramatic	☐	More calm	☐
2	Prefers radical change	☐	Prefers periodic or gradual change	☐
3	Others accommodate you	☐	You accommodate others	☐
4	Actively enrolls others in a cause	☐	Balances leading and following	☐
5	Broadly share your ideas	☐	Keep most opinions to yourself	☐
6	Is comfortable being the center of attention	☐	Prefers to work behind the scenes	☐
7	Prefers risk	☐	Prefers caution	☐
8	Dreamer	☐	Realist	☐
9	Ignores rules	☐	Follows rules	☐
10	Focuses on tomorrow	☐	Focuses on today	☐
	Total		**Total**	
	A. Divided by 2 =		**B. Divided by 2 =**	

SECTION 2 ANSWER: Subtract column B from column A (A minus B) =

1. Count the number of marks in each column.

2. Divide each number by 2.

3. Subtract the result in column B from the result in column A. Write down that number. It may be negative.

Map yourself

1. Use the blank fit matrix in figure 5-2. Start in the center of the grid.

2. Take your section 1 answer. Start at the center of the grid. If your number is positive, move that many steps to the right. If the number is negative, move that many steps to the left. Make a small mark at that point.

3. Now start from the mark you just made. Take your section 2 answer. If your number is positive, move that many steps up. If the number is negative, move that many steps down. Make a small mark at that point.

FIGURE 5-2

Map yourself on the fit matrix

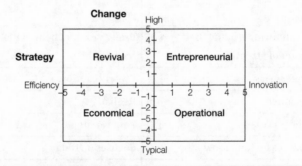

The point where you've mapped yourself suggests the type of environment in which you naturally fit best. Companies with challenges in this general area of the grid (don't try to be too precise) will engage and motivate you more than other companies. This mapping process doesn't indicate that you're highly capable in that area, just that you'll likely to feel most engaged there.

SECOND, DETERMINE YOUR COMPANY'S NEEDS. You know that fit describes how well your natural preferences and interests match what your company needs. You understand where you naturally fit; now you need to determine what your company needs from its talent.

Determining your company's needs requires that you know your company's future strategy well enough to map it on the same two dimensions—strategy and change. Future strategy is more important than current strategy because you need to know how you can best fit going forward. There are a few ways to best understand your company and its strategy:

- You're involved enough in your organization's strategy to be able to map it on the matrix.

- You explain the fit matrix to a few key leaders and ask them to map where they see your company three to four years from now.

- If you work in a public company, your company's website likely has an investor relations page that includes presentations or an executive summary of the company's future strategy. Read those presentations and use them to map your company.

Once you've assessed your company's strategy, draw an "F" on the fit matrix at the intersection of your company's future strategy and change choices.

FINALLY, ASSESS YOUR FIT. How close or far is your natural fit from your company's future needs? If you and your company are in the same box, you're well positioned. If there's any greater distance between you and your company's future position on the matrix, it may be more challenging for you to be a high performer. That doesn't mean you can't be one, but merely that you'll need to apply more effort to ensure that you're seen as, and perform like, someone who's a naturally great fit.

If there's a gap between your company's future location and your natural fit, I suggest ways to close those gaps (see figure 5-3). While you may need to learn or sharpen some skills to improve your fit, you'll see that changing your behaviors is all that's required in many situations. Don't worry if those new behaviors aren't your natural ones. Step six explains how to and why it's fine to fake them.

Manage Your Fit to Maximize Your Performance

Your company likely doesn't assess your fit, so you can improve yourself and your team by applying this simple methodology. If you've taken the fit survey, you'll know where you stand, so try this approach in your next development conversation with your manager:

1. Share your insights about your company. Tell your manager about your assessment of the company's direction and the implications for you.

   – "Hi, Jill, it feels like our [company, group, or division] is in the [entrepreneurial, operational, economical, or revival] phase right now and for the next few years. Given that, when I assess what our company needs from leaders over the next twenty-four months, it seems that we will value leaders who can do _____, _____, and _____. There are certainly many other skills and behaviors that are needed, but these feel more important than others. Do you believe that's an accurate assessment?"

2. Share your insights about yourself. Tell your manager where you believe you fit and why.

   – "I see myself as the best fit in an [entrepreneurial, operational, economical, or revival] environment, which means that my capabilities are generally a [good fit or challenging fit] for our strategy. Do you agree with my assessment?"

3. **Share your plan.** Share how you would like to grow and develop given what the company needs from its leaders.

   – If you're a good fit. "I'd like to keep my development focus on _____ and try to show these skills by doing _____."

   – If you're a challenging fit. "Because the company's focus is changing, I want to make sure that my skills and behaviors change to best support it. I believe I should focus on improving my capabilities for _____, _____, and _____, by doing _____ and _____."

4. **Ask for advice.** Ask your manager for any guidance they can give you about the company's changes or your own development.

   – "What else I should do either in addition to or instead of the activities I suggested?"

Wrapping Up

Fit is a powerful factor in your quest for great delivery and high performance. It's the only one of the eight steps that relies on something that you can't directly control. However, if you assess your fit and adapt your behaviors and capabilities to what your company demands, you'll be able to sustainably perform at a level that few can match.

When you're not a natural fit with your company, you must learn when and how to "fake" the behaviors your company needs. Step six, "fake it," tells you how to do that and why faking it, at times, is far superior to being the genuine you.

FIGURE 5-3

How to close the gaps

Revival

- Let's face it, something's gone wrong to put your company in this space. Recognize that major, transformational changes will happen to your business that may negatively affect some of your coworkers. These changes are necessary to sustain your firm, as painful as some of those decisions may be to you.

- **If you're lower in change:** Don't slow your decisions because they may be difficult to make. Help others to understand the need to move to the future state and the benefits once the company achieves these changes. Because you can better understand how lower-change people will react, offer to help your company's change or communication teams create messages that best explain what's happening and why.

- **If you're strong in innovation:** These difficult changes can fund the growth and innovation that you value. You recognize that changes need to be made and that it will be messy when they happen. You can help identify which projects really need investment this year and which can wait for recovery. You may be better than others at generating new ideas, so volunteer to help groups to develop ideas that accelerate the turnaround.

Entrepreneurial

- It's exciting to create new products and services, but innovation naturally comes with instability and uncertainty. The risks that your company takes here, whether on products, services, geographies, or technology, will be the ones that decide its future for years to come.

- **If you're strong in efficiency:** Innovation can be messy and inefficient, so your skills to organize and structure can support innovation. Offer to support any large-scale project management or implementation processes where your skills will be highly valued. Ensure that company leaders see you as wanting to help the company advance, not serving as the voice of caution.

- **If you're strong in operations:** The organization will naturally evolve to your strong suit—a more disciplined delivery of your products or services. Stay calm and help the company start to build the infrastructure you know it will eventually need. Recognize that entrepreneurs often perceive process as an excuse for bureaucracy and complexity, so be sure you present an exceptionally clear business case for your actions and keep proposed promises simple.

Efficiency

- In companies with an efficiency focus, it's all about expanding the bottom line. Discipline, precision, and control will be far more valued than wild-eyed ideas about new products or markets. Recognize that some innovation will help ensure that your efficient product or service remains differentiated enough to attract customers.

- **If you're strong in entrepreneurial:** Use your bias for speed and action to ensure that projects move at the right pace, without analysis paralysis. Acknowledge your more creative edge in meetings, and frame ideas as "another option you might want to consider" rather than "why aren't we moving faster, investing more, etc."

- **If you're strong in revival:** There's a time to drive change and a time to let processes run for a while. You likely see improvement opportunities around most corners, so be careful how you select and advance those in this environment where there's little or no desire for rapid change. Your action bias will serve you well when you find projects that the company truly values.

Operational

- In this steady state, profits are made and the organization moves with a predictable rhythm. The environment is great for sustained success but can lead to complacency when companies slide toward the middle, not investing enough in innovation.

- **If you're strong in revival:** Don't let the lack of drama and change get you down. As someone who understands how to make smart, tough choices, you can advise on how to best invest for growth, how to prioritize projects, and which talent has the capabilities to thrive in this environment. Even in a steady state, things go wrong, so offer to apply your turnaround skills to even the smallest project to stay visible and fresh.

- **If you're strong in efficiency:** The savings you generate through efficiencies fund the innovation in this space. Be sure that you understand company processes and that you offer suggestions for reducing time and cost, and increasing quality. Recognize that budget dollars might not always flow to your priorities but that your company will win only if every investment brings new creative products and services.

What Can Get in the Way

- I work for one of many business units in my company. Should I fit with that business unit or with the company strategy? You should try to fit with the unit where you work. The purpose of maximizing your fit is to behave and engage in a way that shows you're highly valuable to the company. While it doesn't hurt to be aware of the challenges or opportunities in other business units, the most direct way you can show high performance is to show that you fit well in your current role.

- I can't be genuine or authentic if I have to behave or think in a way that's not really me. I debunk the authenticity movement in step eight, but, for now, consider that there's a set of capabilities and behaviors that your employer needs from you. You have complete freedom to decide if you want to demonstrate those capabilities and behaviors. You may believe that what your company wants is the right thing or the wrong thing, but recognize that your employer simply needs those results. If you don't want to deliver what your company needs because you wouldn't feel genuine doing it, then you should find a new employer where you fit better. If you want to be a consistently high performer, you recognize that employees need to flex with their company's changing needs.

- If I admit to my manager that I'm not a good fit, aren't I risking my job? You should tell your manager that you want to make sure you're a high performer by always adapting to changes in the company strategy. Present your analysis and your plan for closing any gaps. If you don't mention it, your manager will draw his or her own conclusions about your fit with the future and, without your input, may come to a very different decision.

- How accurate do I have to be in mapping my fit or my company's fit? The fit matrix is a guide to help you think about how closely aligned you are (or aren't) with the business strategy. You should assess how close or far you and the company are from each other on the matrix. The greater the distance, the more difficulty you have adjusting your behaviors and skills. If you and your company are in the same quadrant, you're a good fit. If you're less than a half grid away from your company, the behavior and skill changes are within range. If you're more than a half grid apart, and the company will likely be in that position for years, you should ask yourself if you'll be engaged in that environment.

- Isn't it the company's responsibility to help me understand how I fit and how to change? High potentials take accountability for their own success and don't hope their company will recognize their capabilities. Also, many companies aren't sophisticated enough in how they assess people to understand who fits best today and in the future. When you take responsibility to understand how you best fit and make changes to improve it, you're taking charge of your career.

- Doesn't a company perform better when it has different types of team members? This would suggest any place on the matrix could be a good fit. While there's a belief that diverse teams make better decisions, the facts are far more complex. Diverse teams generate more and better choices for the team to make—that's positive. They also make slower decisions and have more conflicts—that's not as good.[12] So, if you want to move fast, a less diverse team will accelerate your progress (even if in the wrong direction). If you want to make safer decisions, a more diverse team is your best choice.

Remember and Apply

The science says:

- Companies change faster than people do, and they require different capabilities than their leaders as they change.

- When you fit better with a company's strategy and change needs, you will be more engaged and a higher performer.

- We each fit best in different company scenarios due to our personality, career path, and personal preferences; none of us is the best fit in every scenario.

You should:

- Understand where you naturally fit in a company's life cycle.

- Understand where your company will be three to five years from today on the fit matrix.

- Learn and demonstrate the capabilities and behaviors needed to perform well in that future state.

Try using:

- Fit matrix and fit matrix assessment to understand your natural fit and how closely it fits with what your company needs

Step 6

Fake It

A ctor Adrien Brody sacrificed his health, girlfriend, and lifestyle to realistically portray Wladyslaw Szpilman in the 2002 movie *The Pianist*. The movie tells the story of Szpilman's terrifying experience in the Warsaw ghetto during World War II as he tries to survive Germany's attempts to exterminate Jews. To ensure he could faithfully represent on screen the horrors and isolation that Szpilman experienced in life, the six-foot-one Brody reduced his weight to 130 pounds, sold his apartment, left his girlfriend, threw away his cell phone and television, and interacted with very few people.

Brody practiced the piano four hours each day so that he could realistically portray his character's virtuosity. He became such an accomplished pianist through this effort that the movie features a difficult Chopin passage played by Brody himself rather than a professional pianist. Brody said that his experience preparing for and acting in *The Pianist* was so emotionally draining that it took him more than a year to recover from it. Brody earned an Oscar for his moving and dramatic performance.[1]

Not every actor must fully transform himself to successfully play a role, but Brody's determination shows that it's possible to temporarily become someone fundamentally different than you to serve a higher purpose. So, if you're asked to display a few behaviors that aren't completely natural to you for the purpose of being a higher performer, I know you're up to the challenge.

We Don't Always Need to See the Real You

Your friends have never said to you, "I can't wait for the day I can go to work with no makeup, wearing a baggy sweat suit, and telling people what I really think of them. That's the genuine me!" or "Next week, the authentic me will show up at the office, grab control of every project, and gossip endlessly at the coffee machine."

Every day, we "fake it" at work for a very good reason—our companies and coworkers need us to. They don't always need the real us to show up; they often need the stylized version. The good news is that you have complete control to show up in the most productive possible way. The key is to understand which behaviors we need to show when in order to achieve high performance.

Why It Matters

Let's take the emotion out of the term "faking it." A high performer needs to understand and display the few most powerful behaviors needed at that moment. Since you have a preferred way of behaving, you're faking it any time you consciously display a behavior that doesn't agree with your preferences. That's fine. No one is going to watch you demonstrate a great new behavior and say, "That's not the genuine her." They're going to say, "Wow, she's really adaptable!" or "Nice to see that positive change!" Even if you don't fully believe in the behavior you need to show, your job as a high performer is to deliver it more quickly and convincingly than anyone else.

You're also a more accomplished faker than you may think. Your extra loud laugh at the boss's joke? Telling an important peer, "That was a great presentation!" after hearing their long-winded speech? You already understand how to manage impressions. This chapter helps you to manage them in a way that increases your performance. What matters most is to recognize the few, most powerful behaviors or actions to display during typical management challenges—what you may need to fake and when.

As your career evolves, your continued high performance will require you to show new behaviors. How fast you adapt to these behaviors will help differentiate you as a high performer. Some of those behaviors won't come naturally to you, and you may not be fully convinced they're the right way to manage or to work. Those of you who are more introverted may feel anxious drawing attention to yourself. Those who are highly self-resilient may not naturally believe that others need to be coached. Your ability to, as the saying goes, "fake it until you make it" is an essential way to practice the behaviors that will ensure your success going forward. That's why "fake it" is step six to high performance.

It helps that people are very open to having their impressions managed, especially in the direction they desire. They're happy to believe that you now behave more like a manager, have a point of view in team meetings, or think more strategically. Take advantage of their willingness to see you in a different light by behaving in one. Each new behavior moves you closer to your theoretical maximum performance.

What We Know

Some people are more naturally wired to fake it. When considering how to behave in a situation, some people ask themselves, "Who does this situation want me to be and how can I be that person?" Academics call these quick-changing people "chameleons" for obvious reasons. These individuals are primarily concerned with fitting with what others need. There's another group who, in that same situation, would ask themselves, "Who am I and how can I be me in this situation?"[2] If you feel that there's nothing more important than consistently showing the genuine you, you'll find it difficult to be a high performer as your company or challenges change. Research also tells us:

- There's only a little fixed 50 percent in faking. How often you fake behaviors is slightly influenced by your core personality. People who are more extroverted and less calm or self-confident are slightly more likely to naturally fake it. That means that only a few people are naturally better fakers than you and that you directly control how much and how well you fake.[3]

- Men are slightly more willing to fake behaviors than women. There's not a huge difference in how much each sex fakes behaviors at work, but faking is a key part of negotiating and ingratiating yourself with others. Those things are linked to increased ratings, promotion, and pay, which makes faking it a strategy that both sexes should practice often.[4]

- We effectively disguise our true selves when we fake it. People are less accurate in identifying your true personality when you fake a behavior. While that may be the entire point of faking it, it demonstrates that your fake behavior appears real to those who see it. In short, faking works.[5]

Given that your company's needs evolve, that different behaviors are required as you move up in your career, and that sometimes your natural behaviors aren't ideal for every situation, you'll need to fake it more often than you might think. The science says that faking works, so which behaviors should you fake, why, and when?

What to Do

Sometimes in your career you will need to behave outside your preferred style. For example, while some people's personality will allow them to easily emerge as a leader, you might need to actively remind yourself to call attention to your accomplishments. You may need to work harder to allow your team to deliver results rather than trying to do everything yourself. You may need to appear more powerful to secure resources or build relationships.

Your behaviors will help differentiate your success in these scenarios, so it's helpful to know which few behaviors matter most and how to fake them if needed. Based on both science and my work with leaders worldwide, I have found that there are three key scenarios where your fixed 50 percent and personal preferences may require you to fake a different set of behaviors, including:

- You need to emerge as a leader.

- You need to be a more effective leader.

- You need to demonstrate power.

You Need to Emerge as a Leader

Some behaviors allow you to emerge as a leader—to get noticed for your work and to build relationships with important people above you.[6] Other behaviors help you to be an effective leader—to manage teams, create strategy, and drive change. Both behaviors are essential, but you need to emphasize each set at different points in your career.

At the risk of oversimplifying what's required to win in each, there's classic science that says emerging leaders differentiate themselves by building relationships up, down, and across the organization. The same science says that effective leaders differentiate themselves by how well they communicate and manage their teams. Knowing which set of behaviors to show when is essential to be a high performer.[7]

When you're new to a role, new to a company, or just starting your career, "emergence" behaviors are critical to getting noticed as a high performer. These behaviors allow you to emerge as a leader by calling attention to you so that others become more personally and professionally familiar with you. Remember that you can't be an effective leader until you emerge as one. Some fixed 50 percent factors support emerging behaviors, so those with higher conscientiousness, extroversion, and openness have a natural advantage in this area. Even if you aren't naturally wired to show emerging leader behaviors, it's essential that others notice you so that you can compete for your company's limited resources and attention.

If you don't believe that you should have to call attention to yourself and that good work speaks for itself, I urge you to reconsider. Success requires that others know about your good work and that they feel good about you in order for you to emerge and succeed. There are only so many spots in your company's high-potential development class, time on the CEO's calendar, and dollars in the bonus pool. You need to be noticed to get your fair share of each of these.

There are three key behaviors that you should fake to emerge and get noticed as a leader: promoting your ideas, making friends, and showing ambition.

PROMOTE YOUR IDEAS. Good work doesn't get noticed on its own or typically not by enough people to matter. At the heart of emerging as a leader is the requirement that you want your accomplishments to be noticed. You can do this most easily by having a point of view on important topics, a base of facts to justify your opinions, and the courage to speak up and present your point of view. Speaking up and appearing self-confident while doing it is the most consistent predictor of successful emerging. It helps if your ideas are well rounded and prove correct over time, but having and expressing an idea is your first step.[8]

You need some ego to seek recognition of your ideas; there's a tipping point between emergence and arrogance. You should speak up in a meeting when you have a good idea (and maybe even try to think of that good idea in advance), not let others speak over you (this is a particular risk for women), and express that idea with the same confidence with which you'd state your own name.[9] Be careful not to let your image get too far in front of what you can deliver.

MAKE FRIENDS (OR AT LEAST CONTACTS). The right people need to see you at the right time. There are social and business components to doing this well. The social component means that you're visible at company events, have lunch and coffee with your peers and important superiors, and chat with teammates during the day. Think of this as classic extroverted behavior—you're connecting with others, making them feel special, building relationships and networks.[10]

To get noticed, you also need to do well at managing up. You need to make your manager like you by seeking his or her input where possible, doing high-quality work, and asking for the highest-profile assignments. Be sure not to criticize your manager, especially in any area where he or she is proud of accomplishments.[11] This may sound like playing politics or sucking up—it is. You may find these tactics slightly distasteful or not genuine, but it's clear from science and practice that they differentiate those who succeed.

These recommendations may sound similar to those I described in step four, "connect." There's definitely an overlap between a great connecting strategy and a great emerging leader strategy, so you can use some of the same relationship planning and management tools I described in that chapter to help you better emerge.

The good news is that sucking up works, and you're unlikely to overdo it. In his book, Jeffrey Pfeffer recounts an experiment conducted to test how much flattery is too much. The assumption was that a little flattery was good, and that more was better, but that too much would have negative effects on the flatterer. The finding? The curve never leveled off. It turned out that no amount of flattery ever caused the person who was flattered to think worse about the person flattering them.[12]

SHOW AMBITION. As obvious as this may seem, you must demonstrate that you want to succeed and contribute more to your organization to be a high performer. Directly tell your manager that you want to contribute more and that you will deliver, behave, and sacrifice to do so. You need to demonstrate a competitive edge— a passion to win as an individual or to drive your team to bigger results. The obvious path is to deliver very high-quality work, hold your team to incredibly high-performance standards, and call out others who aren't performing to a high-enough standard.

These behaviors will help you emerge, but they're only part of what you need to be a high performer. If you only demonstrate emergence behaviors, you'll eventually be labeled political, egotistical, or an empty suit, and your career progress will slow.[13] Once you're in a middle management or midlevel role in your company, you should start to balance those behaviors with behaviors that show you're an effective leader.

You Need to Be a More Effective Leader

An emerging leader focuses on him- or herself. That's fine to get noticed, but it's a derailer if you want to pivot into roles of greater managerial responsibility. An effective leader subsumes his ego and shifts focus to getting bigger results through and with others. Many leaders naturally gravitate to more traditional manager behaviors. But, if you're trying to rapidly move from being an emerging leader to an effective one, or if you've been an individual contributor for many years, you may need to work extra hard to learn these behaviors.

Effective leaders spend more time on the day-to-day management of the business while building the quality and depth of their team.[14] Three tactics will get you there faster: a clear vision, a talent upgrade, and honest coaching.

TELL A CRISP, CLEAR STORY ABOUT YOUR VISION. A clear vision makes it easier for your team to change and perform at higher levels.[15] At least once a quarter, you should develop and communicate to your team a vision with these three points:

- Crisply describe the future state. The simplest, most straightforward way to communicate this vision is to describe it in a from/to statement. "As a [company, division, or region], we're moving *from* a company that does 'this' for 'these people' in 'this way' *to* a company that does 'this' for 'these people' in 'this way.'" For example, "We're moving *from* being a company that provides technology outsourcing to North American companies by competing on price *to* being an integrated technology transformation consultancy to global companies at a premium price."

- Tell why the future is exciting and necessary. State why that vision describes a better place for the business than where you are today ("we'll be stronger competitors"; "we'll get to do more cutting-edge work"). State why the future isn't just a desirable destination, but a necessary one ("we'll lose market share if we don't"; "we'll likely be bought"; "our type of company won't exist ten years from now").

- Sell the benefits. Your team members are interested in the company's future, but they care about their own future. Describe how their life will be better in the vision that you describe (more opportunities for development, greater pay for higher performers). Recognize that not everyone may like the vision you describe. That's fine. If they clearly understand the vision and they don't like it, they're not the right fit for the future. One benefit of having a clear vision is that it helps people to select into or out of the company.

ASSESS AND UPGRADE YOUR TALENT. Effective leaders understand that better-quality talent delivers better business results, and they invest the time to build high-quality teams. An exercise I use when teaching high-potential managers how to get more from their team members is called buy/sell/hold. It's based on what the head of trading at a major investment bank told me many years ago when I offered him a complicated way to analyze talent: "Marc, I analyze my team the same way I analyze my portfolio. Every day I look at each position and ask myself whether I want to increase, decrease, or not change my level of investment. Any day that I don't make a change, I'm saying that I'm happy with that portfolio—that there's no better return that I can achieve. I do the exact same thing with my team." Let's do that exercise. If you manage others, write the names of your team members on a sheet of paper. After each name, write a B, S, or H for whether you'd like to buy (invest more), sell (invest less or get rid of), or hold (maintain the same level of investment) that person. You likely know what needs to change on your team, and this exercise makes it clearer. If your ratings are all buys, then you either have a very unusual team or you need to raise your standards. Try asking one of your peers to rate your team on the same criteria and see if they have a different opinion.

PROVIDE BRUTALLY HONEST COACHING. As human beings, we're hardwired to get along with others, so being brutally honest with someone typically feels uncomfortable. Doing it well is also a hallmark of leaders who create high-performing teams. You want to tell each of your team members one unique thing that you know will improve their performance. List your team members and write that one unique item after each member's name. Schedule a thirty-minute meeting with each within the next two weeks. Give them feedforward about the item and specific ways in which they can practice getting better at it. Let them know that this behavior will help them unlock higher performance.

As you shift to effective leader behaviors, you may worry that you won't be fairly recognized if your team delivers results instead of you. But it's very likely that if your team delivers great results, you'll personally be seen as a high performer.

Why can't a manager exhibit both emerging and effective behaviors? Research shows less than 10 percent of managers score high in both areas. The few in that elite group simply demonstrate the characteristics of both categories at a moderate level.[16] It's certainly possible for anyone to do this, but it takes significant effort to act in a way that's simultaneously consistent and inconsistent with your core personality.

You Need to Demonstrate Power

Power is the ability to change others' well-being, finances, and attitudes. Sometimes you need to exert power to succeed in your organization, but power isn't available to you at a moment's notice. You must cultivate it over time. You should start building power now, because you will absolutely need it at some point in your career.

Lyndon Johnson mastered the capability to acquire and wield power, but it can be a struggle for many of us. I'm personally uncomfortable acting this way. An executive coach gave me great advice when I was in my most recent corporate role. As I complained about the political nature of the company I worked in, he told me that politics was the game being played and that I was a player in that game. If you don't want to play the game, he said, step out of it. If you want to win, he said, you must master the rules of the game and play by them.

Whether it's played openly or subtly, power is the game at your company. You may find it difficult to fake acting with power, but if you want to obtain status or resources, you need to display this essential behavior. Three steps will get you more power, more quickly: being visible, managing up, and making your boss happy.

BE CONSISTENTLY VISIBLE. An amazingly simple and effective insight can help you gain power—show up. And then show up again (and again). A phenomenon called the "mere exposure effect" proves that the more familiar you are to someone, the more positively they think about you. People feel that familiar things are less likely to surprise them, which appeals to their risk-averse nature.[17] The more often someone sees you, hears you, reads about you, and interacts with you, the more you're building your potential power to influence them.

You become more visible in obvious ways: Speak up (productively) in meetings. Have coffees and lunches with peers and superiors. Travel with your boss. Get assigned to important projects.

MANAGE UP. You read earlier that flattery and ingratiation were great strategies to help you emerge as a leader. They work here for the same reasons they work there: flattering people makes them like you more, and the more they like you, the more power (control, budgets, projects) they're willing to trust you with.[18] Managing up is similar to being visible, but you demonstrate it in a different way. Being visible is a broad approach to gaining power—you're generally noticed by many people. Managing up is about being specifically noticed by a select few.

To manage up well, identify the few people with the power and resources to make your career more successful. Your direct manager is one, but you need to identify three or four others. If you've been in your organization for a while, these people may be obvious, but if not, ask others for their insights. Ask your boss, "Are there some senior leaders in the organization it would be helpful for me to get to know better?" Ask your peers, "Who do you think will move fastest into the executive team?"

Once you've identified these leaders, ask them to coffee or lunch with a specifically stated agenda. If your boss has said you should get to know someone, ask her or him to send a quick note of introduction to the person saying that the two of you should connect. If you're working on a project where that person is a sponsor, ask them if you can run a few ideas by them. For nearly any executive, you can let them know you're trying to plan your career or to decide your next move within the company. Say that you would value their input because of their experience and their insights about the company. If you're worried that they may see your actions purely as flattery, remember that the science says it doesn't matter.

MAKE YOUR BOSS VERY HAPPY. Your boss is in the best position to give you power, and you want to perform strongly in the areas that he or she cares most about. You know from the science that even if your performance is weak, your boss will see you more positively if you have a strong relationship. Ask him regularly what areas matter most to him. Ask for guidance on projects or assignments in ways that demonstrate your competence but allows him to feel important. Speak positively about him to others, and he'll hear about it through the back channels at your company. The same will be true if you speak negatively about him.[19]

If you allow yourself to fake it, you can demonstrate high-performing behaviors in the situations where they matter most. This means that you may not be consistently showing the genuine you. That's fine. You show others a consistent high performer instead.

Wrapping Up

Two performance factors you can't fake are sleep and exercise. While there's no shortage of internet wisdom on these topics, a high performer only cares about what's scientifically proven to work. Step seven, "commit your body," tells you what's proven to help and what doesn't matter.

What Can Get in the Way

- You're asking me to lie. No, I'm asking you to behave in a way you're not used to that leads to high performance. Unless you fundamentally disagree with those behaviors, you're simply learning to adapt your behavior to the situation, and you can change it back after you've succeeded. If you disagree with the recommended behavior, you should behave in the way you feel will get the best results.

- I'm not really a good actor. How can I fake it well? You might not be perfect the first time, but the first step is to try. The great thing about practice is that it typically makes you better. Stay true to the advice this chapter lays out for each scenario and ask your boss, peers, or direct reports for feedback on whether your behaviors appear as intended. Use the feedforward approach described in step two, "behave to perform," for the best results.

- How can I change these behaviors rapidly? It's tough to learn new behaviors quickly. The more rounds of practice you have with a behavior, the faster you'll learn it (see step three, "grow yourself faster"). Don't worry about becoming great quickly. Focus on the few, most important things you can do in each scenario. That will ensure that even if you're not yet an expert, you'll apply your effort in the right areas.

Remember and Apply

The science says:

- Different types of behaviors will benefit us in different situations.

- We are all capable of changing our behaviors; dramatic changes will require more effort but are still 100 percent possible.

- The shift from behaving like an emerging leader to behaving like an effective leader is especially important to make at the right time.

You should:

- Understand the key behaviors that will most benefit your performance in different scenarios. Forget the genuine you and focus on being the most effective you.

- Recognize that faking it is just part of the behavior change process; it's the first round of practice.

- Assess your career stage, development needs, and environment to see what type of faking will have the largest benefits for you.

Try using:

- Feedforward process to get insights to which behavior changes are most important

Step 7

Commit
Your Body

Y ou're lying on a sandy beach near the historic Hotel del Coronado in beautiful Southern California. Nearby are the friends who've spent the past two weeks with you on the white sand and in the jade-tinted water. It's 3 a.m. You've crawled to this spot after thirty minutes of kneeling in the sand at the wave line, as cold surf pounded your body. You're soaking wet and shivering uncontrollably. Your hands are chapped raw. Every muscle in your body is filled with painful lactic acid from uninterrupted exercise drills over the past sixty hours. You hear a man scream through a bullhorn that you should quit this group—give up—and enjoy the warm coffee and doughnuts waiting for you just a hundred feet away. You've had two hours of sleep in the past three days. What do you do?

If you want to be a US Navy SEAL, you keep going for another two-and-a-half days through even more intense drills with only two hours of additional sleep. Those sleep-challenged SEAL candidates are attending Basic Underwater Demolition/SEAL training (BUD/S), the first step to becoming a member of this elite military special forces team. During the Hell Week section of BUD/S, candidates are tested by five-and-a-half days of cold, wet, brutally difficult operational training on fewer than four hours of total sleep. More than 80 percent of the candidates take the offer of coffee and doughnuts. A select few continue and achieve feats of physical and mental toughness they never imagined possible.

Those who graduate BUD/S training get closer to their theoretical maximum performance than most of us can ever hope to. Their ability to deliver both physically and mentally over five days with almost no sleep suggests that our bodies have far more potential to deliver results under stress than we believe. The question is how can we best use what we know about the human body to achieve high performance.

Why It Matters

Your body plays a critical role in your performance; it's important to eat right, exercise, and get enough sleep. But you're not going to be a high performer just because you get eight hours of sleep, eat a balanced diet, and regularly visit the gym. Your interest should be in how science says you can use your body to perform better at work. Step seven to high performance is to "commit your body."

Surprisingly little science makes a direct link between our bodies and individual high performance at work. The science that does exist says that sleep matters most, exercise has some minor and specific effects, and diet has no direct effect. That doesn't mean that exercise and diet don't matter in your life, but neither has much power to boost your performance at work. For that reason, let's start our discussion with sleep.

It's hard to miss the articles that berate working professionals for their poor sleep habits and encourage them to get eight hours of undisturbed sleep in a cool, dark, pet-free room, with no exposure to electronic devices beforehand. That's an idealistic goal, and undoubtedly the best advice to optimize your sleep, but it's unrealistic for most of us.

High performers need sleep advice that's a bit more nuanced. What's the best sleep strategy to maximize your performance and your time? In other words, if eight hours is ideal for high performance, what happens when you get six hours? Pull the occasional all-nighter? Get low-quality or too little sleep? Those insights allow you to weigh the trade-offs between getting two additional hours to work or play versus a possible decline in performance and behaviors.

What We Know

Given that many of us get less sleep than we think we need, knowing the right amount and how to best counter the effects of too little or poor-quality sleep is an essential high-performance strategy. Very little sleep science explores the practical implications of sleep loss on high performance. Most sleep studies look at how people perform after twenty-four hours of sleep deprivation, not the continuous weeks of five to six hours of sleep that many working professionals face. Despite that imperfect information, there are still practical sleep insights to guide you closer to your theoretical maximum performance level. Let's start with the basics.

Sleep Quality

There are various definitions of sleep quality, but most include how easy it is to fall asleep, the perceived depth of sleep, and the number of times you wake up during sleep.[1] There's only a small relationship between sleep quality and sleep quantity, which means that a great night's sleep depends less on the number of hours than you might think.[2]

QUALITY IMPACTS PERFORMANCE MORE THAN QUANTITY. The negative effects of sleep come more from low quality than low quantity. Low-quality sleep reduces your performance and your perceived job satisfaction and increases how often you think about quitting your job. Low-quantity sleep doesn't cause any of those reactions. That might explain why some people operate fine on five hours a night, and others struggle after eight hours.[3]

BAD MOOD? IT'S SLEEP QUALITY, NOT QUANTITY. That nasty edge you sometimes show? It's much more likely due to your sleep quality than quantity. Sleep quality affects your mood about four times as much as sleep quantity.[4] Science shows that your mood will be better with a shorter period of high-quality sleep than with a longer, frequently interrupted rest.[5]

Sleep Quantity

Despite years of scientific research, there's still no clear agreement on the natural amount of sleep needed. The National Sleep Foundation says it's between six and ten hours, with a preference for seven to nine hours, but other scientists claim that six-and-a-half to seven hours is the sleep sweet spot.[6] A study of people in remote tribes who don't have our hectic lives or device overload finds that they sleep about six hours a night.[7] That seems like a reasonable starting point for how much sleep we naturally require.

SLEEP LOSS HURTS YOUR BASIC FUNCTIONS, NOT YOUR EXECUTIVE ONES. One of the most surprising findings about not getting enough sleep is that it hurts your basic skills more than your advanced ones. You may think that being sleepy will dull your ability to engage in complex conversations or tasks, but that it won't hurt your ability to drive to the office or remember your best clients' names. The true impact of sleep loss is the exact opposite, and knowing that can help you to develop a great sleep strategy. The conclusive science shows that your more basic capabilities fail first with sleep loss, while your higher-order capabilities remain relatively strong. That means the danger of short-term lack of sleep isn't that you'll blow the big presentation; it's that you'll wreck your car on the way to the big presentation because you've nodded off.

Even if your higher-order capabilities are relatively strong with less sleep, they're not at full strength. Your creative problem solving will decrease, you'll be less innovative, you'll be moodier, and your communication skills will suffer with fewer hours of sleep.[8] These findings are from studies of people who had been awake twenty-four hours, so the effects won't be as dramatic if you've only had one night's poor sleep.

YOU'RE NOT FINE WITH FIVE HOURS EVERY NIGHT. Some people claim their regular schedule involves just four to five hours' sleep, including Martha Stewart, Donald Trump, and historical figures like Thomas Edison. If their claims are true, they're the exception. Only about 5 percent of people can fully function on less than six hours of sleep per night.[9] Even if you want to regularly sleep less, it's challenging. Our genes control our preferred wake time within about one hour, so it's difficult to train ourselves to sleep much less than our body naturally demands.[10]

What to Do

High performers need to answer three questions to determine the right amount of sleep for peak performance and how to best compensate when they don't get enough.

1. How do I get the right quality and quantity of sleep?

There's still no scientific way to determine the right amount of sleep we need. If you consider that science says a ten-minute nap can "replace" one hour's sleep, then six to seven hours of sleep (with a nap) is a reasonable starting point.[11] That amount of sleep each night may build a small sleep debt during the week, but you can pay that back with two extra hours each night on the weekend. If you dip a little in sleep quantity during the week, don't worry. The science says that a few nights with five hours' sleep doesn't substantially reduce your capabilities versus getting a few nights with seven hours' sleep.[12]

The best advice for getting high-quality sleep may sound familiar; it also sounds as if you must be a monk to achieve it. Try to work the following recommendations into your sleep routine, in this order:

- Find and stick to a sleep schedule. Go to sleep and wake up at consistent times every day. Your brain operates in a rhythm, and changing sleep or wake times confuses it and can make you feel sleepy, even with high-quality sleep.

- No caffeine within six hours of bedtime. That caffeine kick stays in your body longer than you realize (it takes about five to six hours to reduce its power by 50 percent).[13] If your last cup is at 6 p.m., you'll still feel some effects at midnight. You might say, "I can fall asleep instantly, even after a double espresso," but that's how fast you fall asleep, not the quality of your sleep. And low-quality sleep makes you much more likely to be a moody jerk the next day.[14]

- No alcohol within three hours of bedtime. Like caffeine, alcohol plays with your natural sleep cycle because it warms your body and puts you into a deep sleep rather than a recovery-boosting REM sleep.

- Have a higher-carb meal closer to bedtime. A higher-carbohydrate meal within four hours of bedtime helps you fall asleep more quickly.[15]

All that science is enlightening and helpful in theory, but challenging to apply in reality. You might not hit your ideal sleep number or you might toss and turn for eight hours, so your sleep quality is low. Science has an answer for that as well and tells you how to maintain a competitive edge, even when sleep challenged.

2. When my sleep quality is low (or I know it will be low), how do I ensure strong performance the next day?

Even with less than optimal sleep quality, you can keep your performance high if you take these simple, controllable steps.

- Self-awareness. Recognize that you're likely to be in a worse mood with low sleep quality. Any negative thoughts (I'm not appreciated; I don't like my job, etc.) will happen more often. On days when your sleep quality is low, tell yourself as you walk through your office's front door, "This is a reminder that you didn't sleep well, so make sure you behave and interact in a positive way today." In addition to self-awareness, let a few others who are close to you (your assistant, best office friend, etc.) know that you had a bad night's sleep and ask them to tell you if you're moody or behaving in a less than ideal way. That's one difference between a high performer and others—you recognize and correct for a weakness; you don't expect others to excuse you for it.

- Food. Low blood sugar can make you even more moody, so keep that level stable all day to help fight the negative effects of low sleep quality. The science of food nutrition says that a high-carb and high-fiber breakfast works best for this and will prevent you from eating too much during the day.[16] If that meal sounds unappetizing, think oatmeal, not dry multigrain toast. Not a breakfast person? Fine. Pay close attention to the earlier discussion of caffeine and recognize that if you take more than your normal dose of caffeine to fight the sleepiness, it can potentially make you even more moody.

- Intense morning exercise. As described in the upcoming exercise section, the best sleep-fighting benefits from exercise come from more intense, longer workouts, but they only help on the same day that you exercise. The good news is that exercise doesn't only help you; it helps your boss too. One study showed that supervisors are less abusive when they get exercise in the morning.[17]

3. When my sleep quantity is low (or I know it will be low), how do I ensure strong delivery the next day?

Since we know that fewer hours of sleep affect our basic functioning a lot and our advanced functioning a little, what's the best strategy to improve each? Thankfully, scientists have studied the exact question of which of two common remedies help sleep-deprived people more—a nap or caffeine. Science says their power to reduce the effects of sleep loss follows this order:

- Naps. Naps are the absolute best way to make up for a lack of sleep and keep your performance level higher than your naturally sleep-deprived state. In realistic experiments, researchers restricted participants to five hours of sleep and then had them take naps of between thirty seconds and thirty minutes. It turns out that a ten-minute nap is optimal and that shorter or longer naps don't increase your awareness or cause you to feel more awake.[18] A nap is far more effective than caffeine if your goal is performance, not just staying alert.[19]

- Caffeine. Think of caffeine more as a safety enhancer than a performance enhancer. The science is clear that fewer hours of sleep hurt basic brain functions (alertness, reaction speed, attention) more than advanced ones. Those are the exact functions that caffeine improves the most.[20] Of all possible foods, only caffeine directly affects performance with clear, broad-based benefits like faster reaction time, decreased fatigue, mood improvement, better working memory, and more. You won't be a better salesperson, programmer, or manager after caffeine, but you'll be awake, aware, and more able to function during the day. The recommended amounts to get those benefits are one to eight cups of tea or one to four cups of coffee a day.[21]

Keep in mind that chronic sleep deprivation exacerbates everything, from diabetes to obesity to car accidents. No solution presented here is intended to substitute for getting a good night's sleep as frequently as possible.

Exercise and Performance

You've heard this one your entire life—diet and exercise, diet and exercise—and it's great advice if you want to live a long and healthy life. The key question is whether there's any evidence that diet and exercise can help improve your performance at work.

While sleep gives you direct and meaningful performance benefits, exercise turns out to have much smaller and mainly long-term effects. It's not that exercise doesn't matter, but unlike sleep, missing a little won't obviously or immediately hurt your performance. The science says:

- Exercise helps most with executive functions. Executive functions don't help make you an executive; they help you to plan, to manage yourself, and to pursue goals. That's good news, since those functions drive high performance. Exercise can provide a limited boost to these but there's no significant exercise effect on your brain's more basic functions.[22]

- You won't remember more with exercise. You can moderately improve your memory by exercising that same day, but long-term exercise only slightly increases short-term memory and doesn't affect long-term memory at all.[23]

- Exercise creates a virtuous cycle. People who are more physically fit get the most performance benefits from exercise, but those with moderate fitness levels don't benefit at all. Those with poor fitness levels actually see lower executive functioning when they exercise.[24]

- Longer exercise helps more. Any exercise of less than twenty minutes produces no same-day performance benefits and exercise of less than eleven minutes hurts your same-day executive functioning.

- More-intense exercise matters more, but only in the morning. Very hard exercise has twice the brain benefit of moderate exercise. Aerobic and resistance exercises combined are much more beneficial than aerobic alone.[25] Curiously, only morning exercise produces measurable, same-day performance benefits.[26]

So what can you do to enhance your performance with exercise?

- Intense exercise—aerobic and weights. A meta-analysis showed that executive functioning was higher the same day if someone had at least twenty minutes of intense exercise that included aerobic and resistance training. Light exercise (i.e., fifteen minutes jogging on the treadmill) didn't have that effect, and doing either aerobic or resistance workouts alone weren't as helpful as doing them together.[27]

- Combine exercise and caffeine. Exercise doesn't have any effect on your basic brain functions, so you'll get the best performance results if you incorporate exercise and caffeine to juice your basic and advanced capabilities.

Diet

Like exercise, a healthy diet provides many long-term benefits, but no science suggests that any specific set of foods or diet routine leads directly to higher performance at work. Only caffeine provides consistent, proven, performance benefits, though other legal substances, including prescription drugs and supplements, are scientifically proven to boost your mental performance. My advice is to focus on the eight steps first.

Wrapping Up

How you manage your body is a completely controllable factor, but one that primarily prevents decreased performance rather than boosting it. Some of the facts about sleep and exercise may be familiar to you, but high performers need to be more strategic in how they apply them. Your great performance, investment in your personal growth, and stellar behaviors can all be undercut if your sleep strategy fails. Fortunately, the science doesn't say that high performance requires Olympian levels of exercise or teenage-quality sleep. Six or seven hours of sleep in a cool, quiet room and some intense morning exercise should deliver the goods.

You now know the seven steps that create a direct, controllable path to high performance. There's just one more thing to do—don't mess it up by falling for a performance-sapping management fad. Those fads come from both well-intended and less-well-intended sources, but they share the common denominator of hurting your ability to be a high performer. In step eight, "avoid distractions," you'll learn which of the most popular fads you should ignore.

What Can Get in the Way

You control how much time you sleep and how often you exercise, so there are no questions and answers for this chapter. If you need detailed advice about better sleep strategies, you can find the best insights at the website for the National Sleep Foundation at www.sleepfoundation.org.

Remember and Apply

The science says:

- Sleep quality matters more than sleep quantity; six to seven hours is the sleep sweet spot.

- Lower-order skills fail first when you don't get enough sleep.

- Naps and caffeine are scientifically proven to partially make up for low sleep quality and quantity.

You should:

- Follow the National Sleep Foundation (https://sleep foundation.org/) guidelines for getting good quality and quantity of sleep.

- Let others at work know when you've had a bad night's sleep, not as an excuse for your behaviors, but so they can remind you to behave well.

- Use one ten-minute nap (where possible) and caffeine to temporarily make up for low sleep quality or quantity.

- Do an intense morning workout to slightly boost your performance during the day and partly make up for low sleep quality.

Step 8

Avoid Distractions

B eing a high performer would be easier if the contents of every best-selling management book and popular TED talk were true. You could then experience unheard-of success if you read the *Wall Street Journal*'s top-ten business best sellers and did exactly what each book said. Unfortunately, no one shares which of those books and talks are filled with truth, which are filled with unproven advice, and which are scientifically proven to be wrong. Until now.

The final step on your journey to high performance is to avoid the fads that distract you from what's scientifically proven to improve your performance. Many of these fads present advice that would seem to make your life easier (focus on your strengths), quickly increase your performance (adopt a growth mindset), or give you instant self-confidence (strike a power pose). They're well marketed, often by a charismatic professor from a reputable business school in a stereotypical TED talk. They often have a scientific paper to back their claims, but those scientific findings are soon proven to be overblown (emotional intelligence), the relabeling of an existing concept (grit), or simply false (power posing, again).

Why It Matters

Your hard work to be a high performer shouldn't be derailed by popular but questionable management advice. Not only will these fads not help you to approach your theoretical maximum performance, they'll waste valuable time that you could apply to the seven steps that are proven to work. Here's a summary of some popular management fads, where they're wrong, and what you should do instead.

What (Not) to Do

A high performer should carefully evaluate any concept that's marketed as a quick and easy way to improve performance. Use the "research, science, or conclusive science" screen before you believe any claims, because those that sound too good to be true typically are. That includes the following claims.

(Please Don't) Focus On Your Strengths

Gallup has sold millions of books that claim you'll be more successful if you focus on what you're good at or hope to be good at. It calls these things your "strengths." The concept that you should focus on your strengths seems like a wonderful recipe to be happy at work. You don't have to confront any hard truths about what's holding you back or risk failure by trying something new. However, those who suggest a strengths focus offer no scientific proof that people perform at a higher level or develop more effectively if they do this. I've asked leaders of Gallup's strengths group to provide some scientific evidence to support their approach. They have more than ten years of data from their strengths tools, but they said they had no scientific evidence that would prove its effectiveness.

On the other hand, there is research that shows: (1) the behaviors we need to succeed as we move up in an organization change, so today's strengths may be irrelevant tomorrow; (2) we have fewer strengths than we think we do (if we define a strength as being meaningfully better at something than others); and (3) our weaknesses (the "derailers" described in step two, "behave to perform") will slow or stop our career progress.[1] Focusing on your strengths will help you be better at the exact same things you're good at today, but won't help you be good at anything else.

WHAT TO DO INSTEAD. Your strengths are your strengths because of your personality, career path, and interests—they'll never stop being your strengths. If you turn up the dial higher and higher on them, you'll create derailers (remember, from step two, "behave to perform," that a strength turned up too high is a derailer). Keep listening to others about the skills and behaviors that you should improve to be more successful. They'll be happy to find a few non-strengths for you to focus on. Step two tells you how to easily gather their input and use it to quickly change your behaviors.

Emotional Intelligence Doesn't Predict Leadership Success

It's a wonderfully intuitive idea that our performance might improve if we better manage our emotions and more accurately perceive others' emotions. What's often sold as emotional intelligence (EI) is almost entirely from the fixed 50 percent factor of personality and does not predict job performance any better than personality does.[2] Leading personality scientist Tomas Chamorro-Premuzic commented that EI had simply repackaged very unsexy elements of personality in a nicer wrapper, saying, "[E]ven if EQ [emotional quotient] is largely old wine in a new bottle, at least the wine is very drinkable."[3]

Turning up the dial too high on EI can even create a condition called psychopathy, where you're so insightful about others' emotions that you become manipulative and superficial.[4] EI can make up for lower IQs in some situations, but if you're missing IQ points, you have a much larger performance challenge ahead.[5]

WHAT TO DO INSTEAD. It is helpful to understand how people see you manage your own and others' emotions and to correct any harmful behaviors. Doing each of these things well enough to be successful isn't a different type of intelligence than IQ. It's just about behaving in a way that your peers and coworkers value. As you read in step two, there are people who are very successful despite what appear to be lower levels of EI. Follow the process defined in step two to get direct or indirect feedback on the areas that your trusted colleagues would most like you to change.

Ten Thousand Hours of Practice Is Exhausting and Irrelevant

I highlighted this finding in the introduction, but let's put the final nail into the "practice" coffin. The myth that anyone can master a skill if they put in ten thousand hours of practice gained traction in Malcolm Gladwell's book *Outliers*. Science says it's simply not true. In studies of chess players and musicians, research shows that hours of practice account for only about one-third of someone's performance.[6] Other science shows that Olympic athletes and chess masters far outperformed their peers even as children, before they could accumulate many hours of practice.[7] That means that practice helps, but it's not the magical solution to performance that some claim it to be.

WHAT TO DO INSTEAD. Recognize that natural talent plus lots of practice will produce great results. No natural talent plus lots of practice will produce a reasonable weekend backhand or jump shot.

You Won't Develop Grit by Reading a Book

Another best-selling book and popular TED talk focuses on something called "grit," which the author claims is a new factor she identified that drives high performance. She defines grit as a "perseverance and passion for long-term goals."[8] The only problem with that claim is that science shows that grit is almost entirely the well-known personality factor of conscientiousness and is therefore solidly in the fixed 50 percent.[9]

We know that conscientiousness drives performance, so there's nothing new in the author's claims. Your core level of grit (conscientiousness) is fixed, so some people will always be more naturally "gritty" than you. You can certainly try harder to stay focused on tasks and be less distractible, but that tactic is not new and is one that those with lower conscientiousness will find tough to master.

WHAT TO DO INSTEAD. Use the goal-setting tactics described in step one, "set big goals," to focus on your few most important goals. You'll be less distracted if you try to focus on three big promises, not ten. Put clear time boundaries on all goals to focus your attention on their completion and consider adding midpoint measures to all your goals. These will ensure that you're regularly measuring and correcting your progress, which will show up as perseverance.

Behave for Results, Not Necessarily "Authentically"

It seems difficult to argue against being an "authentic leader" if the alternative is to be an "inauthentic leader." Maybe that challenge is what has allowed this idea to gain traction among leaders and consultants.

The concept started with the best-selling book *Authentic Leadership*, which stated that corporate America was in a leadership crisis and that more authentic leaders—open, self-aware, genuine— were needed to bring the country forward. After leading academics at Stanford, INSEAD, and Wharton business schools attacked the concept, the book's author said, "The essence of authentic leadership is emotional intelligence."[10] As you read earlier, that suggests that authentic leadership is built on the already shaky foundation of EI. In addition, an authentic leader wouldn't deliberately fake some leadership behaviors, even though science suggests that it's both possible and desirable to do that as you evolve as a leader.

WHAT TO DO INSTEAD. The advice of "know yourself to be a better leader" is certainly helpful, and you can get there through the activities in step two, "behave to perform." But, don't pretend that the unfiltered you is what people always need to see. It's much better to understand if what people need from you in a situation is different from the genuine you and do your best to perform in that way. Step six, "fake it," provides guidance on why and how to do that.

A Growth Mindset Is Great—for Children

The "growth mindset" concept is the darling of Silicon Valley types who believe that it is the key to success.[11] According to the book *Growth Mindset,* someone with this mental attitude believes that we can always increase our intelligence, while those with a "fixed mindset" believe that we are who we are. If you just change your fixed mindset to a growth mindset, you'll be capable of anything, according to fans of the concept. They also claim that having a growth mindset is the only way to increase performance, even though the author's own research shows that other mindsets work too.[12]

The author's original studies to justify this concept are quite interesting and applicable—to children. The book's primary research was conducted in school classrooms with young children, not on adults with fully formed brains.[13] Children's brains are still pliable and growing, so kids can become more intelligent (increase their IQ) when they're kids, but intelligence becomes largely fixed when you're an adult. No matter how hard adults try to meaningfully increase their IQ at age thirty-five or forty, they can't do it.[14] There's also a fixed 50 percent personality component to whether you naturally have a growth mindset or not.[15] So that, plus an unchanging IQ, means that being able to shift to a growth mindset is a significant challenge and far more difficult than saying "I think I can."

WHAT TO DO INSTEAD. If you want to accomplish more than you thought you could or break through a performance barrier, follow the advice given throughout *8 Steps* and start by setting big, challenging goals. You're not going to become more intelligent because you do this, but you will likely achieve a lot more than if you just try to change your mindset.

Power Posing Is Perhaps the Silliest Management Fad Ever

Launched like so many fads, with a scientific paper and a TED talk, power posing emerged from research that showed a boost of testosterone occurs when someone stands in more aggressive postures. The authors claimed: "High-power posers experienced elevations in testosterone, decreases in cortisol, and increased feelings of power and tolerance for risk; low-power posers exhibited the opposite pattern."[16] In other words, if you just stand the right way, you'll feel ready to take on the world.

That sounds cool, but it's 100 percent untrue, according to one of the article's coauthors, who came clean about the experiment, and to other scientists who tried and failed to replicate the original research.[17] That hasn't stopped more than 16 million people from watching the TED talk, or the power-posing concept from seeping into the category of urban legends.

WHAT TO DO INSTEAD. Just stand any way you want to—it doesn't matter.

What Can Get in the Way

- How can I separate the facts from the fads without a PhD in psychology? I hear this question often; while it's not always easy, there are a few things to try. Start by referring to the framework in the introduction that describes research, science, and conclusive science. That will help you recognize that not all claims by people with a PhD after their names are necessarily true.

   Ask those who make these claims for proof that their concept is scientifically proven, and ignore them if the proof they offer is a reference to name-brand companies ("Google uses this, so it must be right"), to personal experience ("this has worked for me at four different companies"), or to non-scientific articles ("*Vanity Fair* had a great piece on this last month"). Be a skeptical consumer and realize that things that sound too good to be true likely are.

- What's wrong with trying new things? It's great to keep an open mind to potential new ways to increase your performance. Your open mind should also be a skeptical mind that demands proof that something works and perhaps doesn't rush to be the first adopter. We already know so much about human performance that it makes sense to execute what's proven to create high performance, rather than hope that someone will discover a magical new path. That huge body of existing evidence about performance also means that anyone who claims to have discovered something new has a very high bar of proof.

- My company told me to use one of the fads you listed. What should I do? You should be a good corporate citizen and follow along, unless you're in a position to argue against the tool, book, or product. Consider the results of that assessment with a skeptical eye.

CONCLUSION

We each start our path to higher performance at different points. Some of you may have many of the natural performance advantages found in the fixed 50 percent. You were born in a middle- to upper-class household in a developed country, went to quality schools, and had few, if any, significant personal challenges as you grew up. Others may start a full step behind due to family, economic, health, or social challenges, or blatant or subtle discrimination. You can't control anything that happened before this moment, so use your past to fuel your performance journey. While we each start our journey in a different place, you control where you finish.

In the preface I mentioned how wonderful it would be if someone would tell us early in life how to succeed. We've just had that conversation. You now know exactly what's proven to make you a high performer and have the tools and insights you need to successfully apply that advice. The eight steps are clear, powerful, and scientifically proven to work.

I acknowledge that the eight steps are straightforward, but they are not easy. Achieving them will take meaningful effort and personal sacrifice. That's OK. If they were easy, you wouldn't feel quite as good about becoming a high performer. You can complete as many steps as you choose, but recognize that the more steps you take, the more likely you are to improve your performance. You'll see immediate benefits from each step, so I recommend that you choose one today and take action to move forward.

High performance is a choice. Focus on what you can change and ignore the rest!

APPENDIX

To access the following tools, go to the Tools section at www. the8steps.com and enter the password "highperformer."

Introduction: How to Be a High Performer

- Online IQ test link

- *8 Steps* audit

Step 1: Set Big Goals

- Exercise: Combine tasks into goals

- Exercise: Prioritize goals

Step 2: Behave to Perform

- 360-degree assessment example surveys and reports

- Hogan derailer mini-assessment

- Ten-item personality test and key to scoring it (test also included below)

Step 3: Grow Yourself Faster

- Sample experience map

- Personal experience map template

Step 4: Connect

- Connection planning sheet

Step 5: Maximize Your Fit

- Fit matrix assessment

- Fit matrix template

The Ten-Item Personality Inventory

This ten-item, one-minute assessment is scientifically proven to be almost as accurate as a full-length, half-hour personality test.[1] You may want to take it a few times and average your scores to get the most accurate results. This assessment will help you understand your natural tendencies, but don't use the results as an excuse for your behaviors. It will help show you your "natural hair," not the limits of your behavior.

Here are a number of descriptions that may or may not apply to you. Please use the scale to the right and write a number next to each set of words to indicate the extent to which you agree or disagree with that statement. You should rate the extent to which the pair of traits applies to you, even if one characteristic applies more strongly than the other.

I see myself as:

1. _____ Extroverted, enthusiastic

2. _____ Critical, quarrelsome

3. _____ Dependable, self-disciplined

4. _____ Anxious, easily upset

5. _____ Open to new experiences, complex

6. _____ Reserved, quiet

7. _____ Sympathetic, warm

8. _____ Disorganized, careless

9. _____ Calm, emotionally stable

10. _____ Conventional, uncreative

Rate using this scale

1 = Disagree strongly

2 = Disagree moderately

3 = Disagree a little

4 = Neither agree nor disagree

5 = Agree a little

6 = Agree moderately

7 = Agree strongly

How to Score the Assessment

There's a small amount of math, but it's straightforward and follows this pattern:

EXAMPLE: Extroversion:

Write your answer to Q1: 6

Subtract your answer to Q6 from 8: 8 – 4 = 4

Add the two numbers together: 6 + 4 = 10

Divide that number by 2 to get your Extroversion score: 10 ÷ 2 = **5**

Extroversion   = 6

Write your answer to Q1: _____

Subtract your answer to Q6 from 8: 8 – _____ = _____

Add the two numbers together: _____ + _____ = _____

Divide that number by 2 to get your **Extroversion** score:

_____ ÷ 2 = _____

Agreeableness   4.5

Write your answer to Q7: _____

Subtract your answer to Q2 from 8: 8 – _____ = _____

Add the two numbers together: _____ + _____ = _____

Divide that number by 2 to get your **Agreeableness** score:

_____ ÷ 2 = _____

Conscientiousness   5.5

Write your answer to Q3: 5

Subtract your answer to Q8 from 8: 8 – 2 = 6

Add the two numbers together: _____ + _____ = _____

Divide that number by 2 to get your **Conscientiousness** score:

_____ ÷ 2 = 5.5

Emotional Stability   2

Write your answer to Q9: 3

Subtract your answer to Q4 from 8: 8 – _____ = 1

Add the two numbers together: _____ + _____ = _____

Divide that number by 2 to get your **Emotional Stability** score:

_____ ÷ 2 = _____

Openness to Experience

Write your answer to Q5: _____

Subtract your answer to Q10 from 8: 8 – _____ = _____

Add the two numbers together: _____ + _____ = _____

Divide that number by 2 to get your **Openness to Experience** score:

_____ ÷ 2 = _____

Look up your scores at www.the8steps.com and use the Personality Mini-Survey Norms to see how you compare to others.

NOTES

Preface

1. A meta-analysis reviews many different studies that relate to a similar topic. The goal is to see if the conclusion found in each study is relatively similar to the conclusions found in the others. If all of the studies reach a similar conclusion, there's strong proof that the finding is scientifically true.

Introduction

1. Around 25% is intelligence. Frank L. Schmidt and John Hunter, "General Mental Ability in the World of Work: Occupational Attainment and Job Performance," *Journal of Personality and Social Psychology* 86, no. 1 (2004): 162. Approximately 10%–20% are personality factors. Murray R. Barrick, Michael K. Mount, and Timothy A. Judge, "Personality and Performance at the Beginning of the New Millennium: What Do We Know and Where Do We Go Next?," *International Journal of Selection and Assessment* 9, no. 1–2 (2001): 9–30. Up to around 5% are socioeconomic and physical characteristics. Some of those factors are correlated; I cite each individual fact elsewhere in the book.

2. John E. Hunter, Frank L. Schmidt, and Michael K. Judiesch, "Individual Differences in Output Variability as a Function of Job Complexity," *Journal of Applied Psychology* 75, no. 1 (1990): 28.

3. Boris Groysberg, Jeremiah Lee, Jesse Price, and J. Yo-Jud Cheng, "The Leader's Guide to Corporate Culture," *Harvard Business Review,* January–February 2018.

4. Tim Ferriss, "Relax Like a Pro: 5 Steps to Hacking Your Sleep," http://fourhourworkweek.com/2008/01/27/relax-like-a-pro-5-steps-to-hacking-your-sleep/, accessed August 4, 2017; Christopher Shea, "Empty Stomach Intelligence," *New York Times Magazine,* December 10,

2006, http://www.nytimes.com/2006/12/10/magazine/10section1C.t-1.
html?_r=0.

5. Malcolm Gladwell, *Outliers: The Story of Success* (Vancouver: Hachette, 2008).

6. David Z. Hambrick et al., "Accounting for Expert Performance: The Devil Is in the Details," *Intelligence* 45 (2014): 112–114.

7. M. J. Ree and J. A. Earles, "Intelligence Is the Best Predictor of Job Performance," *Current Directions in Psychological Science* 1, no. 3 (1992): 86–89.

8. Joseph D. Matarazzo, *Wechsler's Measure and Appraisal of Adult Intelligence*, 5th ed. (New York: Oxford University Press, 1972).

9. Huy Le et al., "Too Much of a Good Thing: Curvilinear Relationships between Personality Traits and Job Performance," *Journal of Applied Psychology* 96, no. 1 (2011): 113.

10. B. W. Roberts and W. F. DelVecchio, "The Rank-Order Consistency of Personality Traits from Childhood to Old Age: A Quantitative Review of Longitudinal Studies," *Psychological Bulletin* 126, no. 1 (2000): 3.

11. Anne Case and Christina Paxson, "Stature and Status: Height, Ability, and Labor Market Outcomes," *Journal of Political Economy* 116, no. 3 (2008): 499–532; Timothy A. Judge and Daniel M. Cable, "The Effect of Physical Height on Workplace Success and Income: Preliminary Test of a Theoretical Model," *Journal of Applied Psychology* 89, no. 3 (2004): 428.

12. N. Gregory Mankiw and Matthew Weinzierl, "The Optimal Taxation of Height: A Case Study of Utilitarian Income Redistribution," *American Economic Journal: Economic Policy* 2, no. 1 (2010): 155–176.

13. Timothy A. Judge, Charlice Hurst, and Lauren S. Simon, "Does It Pay to Be Smart, Attractive, or Confident (or All Three)? Relationships among General Mental Ability, Physical Attractiveness, Core Self-Evaluations, and Income," *Journal of Applied Psychology* 94, no. 3 (2009): 742; Judith H. Langlois et al., "Maxims or Myths of Beauty? A Meta-Analytic and Theoretical Review," *Psychological Bulletin* 126, no. 3 (2000): 390.

14. Cort W. Rudolph, Charles L. Wells, Marcus D. Weller, and Boris B. Baltes, "A Meta-Analysis of Empirical Studies of Weight-Based Bias in the Workplace," *Journal of Vocational Behavior* 74, no. 1 (2009): 1–10.

15. Aparna Joshi, Jooyeon Son, and Hyuntak Roh, "When Can Women Close the Gap? A Meta-Analytic Test of Sex Differences in Performance and Rewards," *Academy of Management Journal* 58, no. 5 (2015): 1516–1545.

16. Selcuk R. Sirin, "Socioeconomic Status and Academic Achievement: A Meta-Analytic Review of Research," *Review of Educational Research* 75, no. 3 (2005): 417–453.

17. Mark R. Leary, Ellen S. Tambor, Sonja K. Terdal, and Deborah L. Downs, "Self-Esteem as an Interpersonal Monitor: The Sociometer Hypothesis," *Journal of Personality and Social Psychology* 68, no. 3 (1995): 518.

18. W. Keith Campbell and Constantine Sedikides, "Self-Threat Magnifies the Self-Serving Bias: A Meta-Analytic Integration," *Review of General Psychology* 3, no. 1 (1999): 23–43.

19. Jerald M. Jellison and Jane Green, "A Self-Presentation Approach to the Fundamental Attribution Error: The Norm of Internality," *Journal of Personality and Social Psychology* 40, no. 4 (1981): 643.

20. Raymond S. Nickerson, "Confirmation Bias: A Ubiquitous Phenomenon in Many Guises," *Review of General Psychology* 2, no. 2 (1998): 175.

21. V. M. Zatsiorsky and W. J. Kraemer, *Science and Practice of Strength Training* (Champaign, IL: Human Kinetics, 2006). Note: Terminology changed from "maximal" to "maximum" to ease understanding.

Step 1: Set Big Goals

1. Edwin A. Locke, "Toward a Theory of Task Motivation and Incentives," *Organizational Behavior and Human Performance* 3, no. 2 (1968): 157–189.

2. Timothy A. Judge and Remus Ilies, "Relationship of Personality to Performance Motivation: A Meta-Analytic Review," *Journal of Applied Psychology* 87, no. 4 (2002): 797.

3. Edwin A. Locke and Gary P. Latham, "Building a Practically Useful Theory of Goal Setting and Task Motivation: A 35-Year Odyssey," *American Psychologist* 57, no. 9 (2002): 705.

4. Ibid.

5. Camille A. Olson and Gregory M. Davis, "Pros and Cons of Forced Ranking and Other Relative Performance Ranking Systems," *Society for Human Resource Management Legal Report*, March 2003 (citing Hay Group, "Achieving Outstanding Performance Through a 'Culture of Dialogue,'" working paper, 2002).

6. A. N. Kluger and A. DeNisi, "The Effects of Feedback Interventions on Performance: A Historical Review, a Meta-Analysis, and a Preliminary

Feedback Intervention Theory," *Psychological Bulletin* 119, no. 2 (1996): 254–284.

7. Joel Brockner, William R. Derr, and Wesley N. Laing, "Self-Esteem and Reactions to Negative Feedback: Toward Greater Generalizability," *Journal of Research in Personality* 21, no. 3 (1987): 318–333.

8. Marshall Goldsmith, "Try Feedforward Instead of Feedback," *Journal for Quality and Participation* 8 (2003): 38–40.

Step 2: Behave to Perform

1. Eric Krangel, "Mark Cuban: Yahoo Screwed Because Jerry Is 'Too Nice' (YHOO)," *Business Insider*, October 29, 2008, http://www.businessinsider. com/2008/10/mark-cuban-jerry-yang-isn-t-mean-enough-yhoo-.

2. Jay Yarow, "Jerry Yang Is Out," *Business Insider*, January 17, 2012, http://www.businessinsider.com/jerry-yang-is-out-2012-1.

3. "Steve Jobs: A Genius But a Bad, Mean Manager," Inquirer.net, October 25, 2011, http://technology.inquirer.net/5713/steve-jobs-a-genius-but-a-bad-mean-manager.

4. Brad Stone and Claire Cain Miller, "Jerry Yang, Yahoo Chief, Steps Down," *New York Times*, November 17, 2008, http://www.nytimes. com/2008/11/18/technology/companies/18yahoo.html.

5. Timothy A. Judge, Joyce E. Bono, Remus Ilies, and Megan W. Gerhardt, "Personality and Leadership: A Qualitative and Quantitative Review," *Journal of Applied Psychology* 87, no. 4 (2002): 765.

6. Mercer, 2013 Global Performance Management Survey Report, https://www.mercer.com/content/dam/mercer/attachments/global/ Talent/Assess-BrochurePerfMgmt.pdf.

7. Fabio Sala, "Executive Blind Spots: Discrepancies Between Self-and Other-Ratings," *Consulting Psychology Journal: Practice and Research* 55, no. 4 (2003): 222.

8. Scott B. MacKenzie, Philip M. Podsakoff, and Gregory A. Rich, "Transformational and Transactional Leadership and Salesperson Performance," *Journal of the Academy of Marketing Science* 29, no. 2 (2001): 115–134.

9. Robert B. Kaiser and Darren V. Overfield, "Assessing Flexible Leadership as a Mastery of Opposites," *Consulting Psychology Journal: Practice and Research* 62, no. 2 (2010): 105.

10. Kerry L. Jang, W. John Livesley, and Philip A. Vemon, "Heritability of the Big Five Personality Dimensions and Their Facets: A Twin Study," *Journal of Personality* 64, no. 3 (1996): 577–592.

11. Jule Specht, Boris Egloff, and Stefan C. Schmukle, "Stability and Change of Personality across the Life Course: The Impact of Age and Major Life Events on Mean-Level and Rank-Order Stability of the Big Five," *Journal of Personality and Social Psychology* 101, no. 4 (2011): 862.

12. Bernard M. Bass, Bruce J. Avolio, Dong I. Jung, and Yair Berson, "Predicting Unit Performance by Assessing Transformational and Transactional Leadership," *Journal of Applied Psychology* 88, no. 2 (2003): 207.

13. Timothy A. Judge and Ronald F. Piccolo, "Transformational and Transactional Leadership: A Meta-Analytic Test of Their Relative Validity," *Journal of Applied Psychology* 89, no. 5 (2004): 755.

14. The original four factors have been relabeled for ease of understanding. The original labels can be found in Bernard M. Bass and Bruce J. Avolio, *Improving Organizational Effectiveness through Transformational Leadership* (Thousand Oaks, CA: Sage, 1994).

15. Timothy A. Judge and Joyce E. Bono, "Five-Factor Model of Personality and Transformational Leadership," *Journal of Applied Psychology* 85, no. 5 (2000): 751.

16. Steven N. Kaplan, Mark M. Klebanov, and Morten Sorensen, "Which CEO Characteristics and Abilities Matter?," *Journal of Finance* 67, no. 3 (2012): 973–1007.

17. Justin Kruger and David Dunning, "Unskilled and Unaware of It: How Difficulties in Recognizing One's Own Incompetence Lead to Inflated Self-Assessments," *Journal of Personality and Social Psychology* 77, no. 6 (1999): 1121.

18. Marshall Goldsmith, "Try Feedforward Instead of Feedback," *Journal for Quality and Participation* 8 (2003): 38–40.

Step 3: Grow Yourself Faster

1. Sarah Lacy, "Peter Thiel: We're in a Bubble and It's Not the Internet. It's Higher Education," *TechCrunch*, April 10, 2011, https://techcrunch.com/2011/04/10/peter-thiel-were-in-a-bubble-and-its-not-the-internet-its-higher-education/.

2. Thiel Fellowship FAQ page, http://thielfellowship.org/faq/, accessed August 18, 2017.

3. Ivy Coach, 2019 Ivy League Admissions Statistics, https://www.ivycoach.com/2019-ivy-league-admissions-statistics/, accessed August 17, 2017.

4. Michael Gentilucci, "Larry Summers Blasts Thiel Foundation Fellowship: 'Single Most Misdirected Bit of Philanthropy This Decade,'" *Inside Philanthropy*, October 16, 2013, https://www.insidephilanthropy.com/tech-philanthropy/2013/10/16/larry-summers-blasts-thiel-foundation-fellowship-single-most.html.

5. Tom Clynes, "Peter Thiel Thinks You Should Skip College, and He'll Even Pay You for Your Trouble," *Newsweek*, February 22, 2017, http://www.newsweek.com/2017/03/03/peter-thiel-fellowship-college-higher-education-559261.html.

6. Michael M. Lombardo and Robert W. Eichinger, *The Leadership Machine* (Minneapolis: Lominger, 2005).

7. Ilana Kowarski, "Map: Where *Fortune* 100 CEOs Earned MBAs," *US News and World Report*, March 21, 2017, https://www.usnews.com/education/best-graduate-schools/top-business-schools/articles/2017-03-21/map-where-fortune-100-ceos-earned-mbas.

8. Marshall Goldsmith, *What Got You Here Won't Get You There: How Successful People Become Even More Successful* (New York: Profile Books, 2010).

Step 4: Connect

1. "The Capitol's Age Pyramid: A Greying Congress," *Wall Street Journal*, http://online.wsj.com/public/resources/documents/info-CONGRESS_AGES_1009.html, accessed July 25, 2017.

2. Diane Coutu, "Lessons in Power: Lyndon Johnson Revealed," *Harvard Business Review*, April 2006, https://hbr.org/2006/04/lessons-in-power-lyndon-johnson-revealed.

3. Ko Kuwabara, Claudius Hildebrand, and Xi Zou, "Lay Theories of Networking: How Laypeople's Beliefs about Networks Affect Their Attitudes and Engagement toward Instrumental Networking," *Academy of Management Review* 43, no. 1 (2016), doi:10.5465/amr.2015.0076.

4. Bob Morris, "Jeffrey Pfeffer on Leadership BS: An Interview by Bob Morris," *Blogging on Business*, February 28, 2016, https://bobmorris.biz/jeffrey-pfeffer-on-leadership-bs-an-interview-by-bob-morris.

5. Sandy J. Wayne and Robert C. Liden, "Effects of Impression Management on Performance Ratings: A Longitudinal Study," *Academy of Management Journal* 38, no. 1 (1995): 232–260.

6. Neville T. Duarte, Jane R. Goodson, and Nancy R. Klich, "How Do I Like Thee? Let Me Appraise the Ways," *Journal of Organizational Behavior* 14, no. 3 (1993): 239–249.

7. Ralph Katz, Michael Tushman, and Thomas J. Allen, "The Influence of Supervisory Promotion and Network Location on Subordinate Careers in a Dual Ladder RD&E Setting," *Management Science* 41, no. 5 (1995): 848–863.

8. Scott E. Seibert, Maria L. Kraimer, and Robert C. Liden, "A Social Capital Theory of Career Success," *Academy of Management Journal* 44, no. 2 (2001): 219–237.

9. Rob Cross and Jonathon N. Cummings, "Tie and Network Correlates of Individual Performance in Knowledge-Intensive Work," *Academy of Management Journal* 47, no. 6 (2004): 928–937.

10. Cameron Anderson, Sandra E. Spataro, and Francis J. Flynn, "Personality and Organizational Culture as Determinants of Influence," *Journal of Applied Psychology* 93, no. 3 (2008): 702.

11. Samuel Y. Todd, Kenneth J. Harris, Ranida B. Harris, and Anthony R. Wheeler, "Career Success Implications of Political Skill," *Journal of Social Psychology* 149, no. 3 (2009): 279–304.

12. Chu-Hsiang Chang, Christopher C. Rosen, and Paul E. Levy, "The Relationship between Perceptions of Organizational Politics and Employee Attitudes, Strain, and Behavior: A Meta-Analytic Examination," *Academy of Management Journal* 52, no. 4 (2009): 779–801.

13. Edward E. Jones, Lloyd K. Stires, Kelly G. Shaver, and Victor A. Harris, "Evaluation of an Ingratiator by Target Persons and Bystanders," *Journal of Personality* 36, no. 3 (1968): 349–385.

14. John S. Seiter and Eric Dutson, "The Effect of Compliments on Tipping Behavior in Hairstyling Salons," *Journal of Applied Social Psychology* 37, no. 9 (2007): 1999–2007.

15. Elaine Chan and Jaideep Sengupta, "Insincere Flattery Actually Works: A Dual Attitudes Perspective," *Journal of Marketing Research* 47, no. 1 (2010): 122–133.

16. Mark C. Bolino and William H. Turnley, "More Than One Way to Make an Impression: Exploring Profiles of Impression Management," *Journal of Management* 29, no. 2 (2003): 141–160.

17. Alvin W. Gouldner, "The Norm of Reciprocity: A preliminary statement," *American Sociological Review* 25, no. 2 (1960): 161–178.

18. Seibert et al., "A Social Capital Theory of Career Success."

19. Jens B. Asendorpf and Susanne Wilpers, "Personality Effects on Social Relationships," *Journal of Personality and Social Psychology* 74, no. 6 (1998): 1531.

20. Joel M. Podolny and James N. Baron, "Resources and Relationships: Social Networks and Mobility in the Workplace," *American Sociological Review* 62, no. 5 (1997): 673–693.

21. Thomas Gilovich, Victoria Husted Medvec, and Kenneth Savitsky, "The Spotlight Effect in Social Judgment: An Egocentric Bias in Estimates of the Salience of One's Own Actions and Appearance," *Journal of Personality and Social Psychology* 78, no. 2 (2000): 211.

22. Nicholas Epley, Kenneth Savitsky, and Thomas Gilovich, "Empathy Neglect: Reconciling the Spotlight Effect and the Correspondence Bias," *Journal of Personality and Social Psychology* 83, no. 2 (2002): 300.

23. Thomas V. Pollet, Sam G. B. Roberts, and Robin I. M. Dunbar, "Extraverts Have Larger Social Network Layers," *Journal of Individual Differences* 32, no. 3 (2011).

Chapter 5: Maximize Your Fit

1. Richard Foster and Sarah Kaplan, *Creative Destruction: Why Companies That Are Built to Last Underperform the Market—and How to Successfully Transform Them* (New York: Crown Business, 2011).

2. Betsy Morris, "The Real Story: How Did Coca-Cola's Management Go from First-Rate to Farcical in Six Short Years?," *Fortune*, May 31, 2004, 84.

3. Bernard M. Bass, "Two Decades of Research and Development in Transformational Leadership," *European Journal of Work and Organizational Psychology* 8, no. 1 (1999): 9–32.

4. Morris, "The Real Story," 84.

5. Warren Bennis and James O'Toole, "Don't Hire the Wrong CEO," *Harvard Business Review*, May–June 2000, 170–176.

6. Timothy A. Judge, "Person–Organization Fit and the Theory of Work Adjustment: Implications for Satisfaction, Tenure, and Career Success," *Journal of Vocational Behavior* 44, no. 1 (1994): 32–54.

7. Michelle L. Verquer, Terry A. Beehr, and Stephen H. Wagner, "A Meta-Analysis of Relations between Person–Organization Fit and Work Attitudes," *Journal of Vocational Behavior* 63, no. 3 (2003): 473–489.

8. Hao Zhao, Scott E. Seibert, and G. Thomas Lumpkin, "The Relationship of Personality to Entrepreneurial Intentions and Performance: A Meta-Analytic Review," *Journal of Management* 36, no. 2 (2010): 381–404.

9. Robert E. Quinn and Kim Cameron, "Organizational Life Cycles and Shifting Criteria of Effectiveness: Some Preliminary Evidence," *Management Science* 29, no. 1 (1983): 33–51.

10. To say that you want to be the best at both means that you'd have to be more efficient than your most efficiency-oriented competitors and more innovative than your most innovation-oriented competitors to win. That's simply not a sustainable approach over any meaningful length of time. Stewart Thornhill and Roderick E. White, "Strategic Purity: A Multi-Industry Evaluation of Pure vs. Hybrid Business Strategies," *Strategic Management Journal* 28, no. 5 (2007): 553–561.

11. Bass, "Two Decades of Research and Development in Transformational Leadership."

12. Aparna Joshi and Hyuntak Roh, "The Role of Context in Work Team Diversity Research: A Meta-Analytic Review," *Academy of Management Journal* 52, no. 3 (2009): 599–627.

Step 6: Fake It

1. Stephanie Cook Broadhurst, "For This Role, Artist Literally Starved," *Christian Science Monitor*, December 27, 2002, https://www.csmonitor.com/2002/1227/p15s01-almo.html.

2. Mark Snyder, "Self-Monitoring Processes," *Advances in Experimental Social Psychology* 12 (1979): 85–128.

3. Adrian Furnham, "Personality Correlates of Self-Monitoring: The Relationship between Extraversion, Neuroticism, Type A Behaviour and Snyder's Self-Monitoring Construct," *Personality and Individual Differences* 10, no. 1 (1989): 35–42.

4. David V. Day, Deidra J. Shleicher, Amy L. Unckless, and Nathan J. Hiller, "Self-Monitoring Personality at Work: A Meta-Analytic Investigation of Construct Validity," *Journal of Applied Psychology* 87, no. 2 (2002): 390.

5. Murray R. Barrick, Laura Parks, and Michael K. Mount, "Self-Monitoring as a Moderator of the Relationships between Personality Traits and Performance," *Personnel Psychology* 58, no. 3 (2005): 745–767.

6. Fred Luthans, Richard Hodgetts, and Stuart Rosenkrantz, *Real Managers* (Pensacola, FL: Ballinger, 1988).

7. Timothy A. Judge, Joyce E. Bono, Remus Ilies, and Megan W. Gerhardt, "Personality and Leadership: A Qualitative and Quantitative review," *Journal of Applied Psychology* 87, no. 4 (2002): 765.

8. Jeffrey Pfeffer, *Managing with Power: Politics and Influence in Organizations* (Boston: Harvard Business Press, 1992).

9. Christopher F. Karpowitz, Tali Mendelberg, and Lee Shaker, "Gender Inequality in Deliberative Participation," *American Political Science Review* 106, no. 3 (2012): 533–547.

10. Fred Luthans, "Successful vs. Effective Real Managers," *Academy of Management Executive* 2, no. 2 (1988): 127–132.

11. Pfeffer, *Managing with Power.*

12. Jeffrey Pfeffer, *Power: Why Some People Have It—and Others Don't* (New York: HarperBusiness, 2010).

13. Timothy A. Judge and Robert D. Bretz Jr., "Political Influence Behavior and Career Success," *Journal of Management* 20, no. 1 (1994): 43–65.

14. Luthans et al., *Real Managers.*

15. Mark A. Griffin, Sharon K. Parker, and Claire M. Mason, "Leader Vision and the Development of Adaptive and Proactive Performance: A Longitudinal Study," *Journal of Applied Psychology* 95, no. 1 (2010): 174.

16. Luthans, "Successful vs. Effective Real Managers."

17. Angela Y. Lee and Aparna A. Labroo, "The Effect of Conceptual and Perceptual Fluency on Brand Evaluation," *Journal of Marketing Research* 41, no. 2 (2004): 151–165.

18. Chad A. Higgins, Timothy A. Judge, and Gerald R. Ferris, "Influence Tactics and Work Outcomes: A Meta-Analysis," *Journal of Organizational Behavior* 24, no. 1 (2003): 89–106.

19. Pfeffer, *Power: Why Some People Have It—and Others Don't.*

Step 7: Commit Your Body

1. Allison G. Harvey, Kathleen Stinson, Katriina L. Whitaker, Damian Moskovitz, and Harvinder Virk, "The Subjective Meaning of Sleep Quality: A Comparison of Individuals with and without Insomnia," *Sleep* 31, no. 3 (2008): 383–393.

2. Brett Litwiller, Lori Anderson Snyder, William D. Taylor, and Logan M. Steele, "The Relationship between Sleep and Work: A Meta-Analysis," *Journal of Applied Psychology* 102, no. 4 (2017): 682–699.

3. June J. Pilcher, Douglas R. Ginter, and Brigitte Sadowsky, "Sleep Quality versus Sleep Quantity: Relationships between Sleep and Measures of Health, Well-Being and Sleepiness in College Students," *Journal of Psychosomatic Research* 42, no. 6 (1997): 583–596.

4. Litwiller et al., "The Relationship between Sleep and Work."

5. Patrick H. Finan, Phillip J. Quartana, and Michael T. Smith, "The Effects of Sleep Continuity Disruption on Positive Mood and Sleep Architecture in Healthy Adults," *Sleep* 38, no. 11 (2015): 1735–1742.

6. Max Hirshkowitz et al., "National Sleep Foundation's Sleep Time Duration Recommendations: Methodology and Results Summary," *Sleep Health* 1, no. 1 (2015): 40–43.

7. Gandhi Yetish et al., "Natural Sleep and Its Seasonal Variations in Three Pre-industrial Societies," *Current Biology* 25, no. 21 (2015): 2862–2868.

8. Yvonne Harrison and James A. Horne, "The Impact of Sleep Deprivation on Decision Making: A Review," *Journal of Experimental Psychology: Applied* 6, no. 3 (2000): 236.

9. Melinda Beck, "The Sleepless Elite, Why Some People Can Run on Little Sleep and Get So Much Done," *Wall Street Journal*, April 5, 2011, https://www.wsj.com/articles/SB10001424052748703712504576242701752957910.

10. Michael T. Lin et al., M. Flint Beal, and David K. Simon, "Somatic Mitochondrial DNA Mutations in Early Parkinson and Incidental Lewy Body Disease," *Annals of Neurology* 71, no. 6 (2012): 850–854.

11. J. Horne, "The End of Sleep: 'Sleep Debt' versus Biological Adaptation of Human Sleep to Waking Needs," *Biological Psychology* 87, no. 1 (2011): 1–14.

12. Gregory Belenky at al., "Patterns of Performance Degradation and Restoration during Sleep Restriction and Subsequent Recovery: A Sleep Dose-Response Study," *Journal of Sleep Research* 12, no. 1 (2003): 1–12.

13. Ester Zylber-Katz, Liora Granit, and Micha Levy, "Relationship between Caffeine Concentrations in Plasma and Saliva," *Clinical Pharmacology & Therapeutics* 36, no. 1 (1984): 133–137.

14. Christopher Drake, Timothy Roehrs, John Shambroom, and Thomas Roth, "Caffeine Effects on Sleep Taken 0, 3, or 6 Hours before Going to Bed," *Journal of Clinical Sleep Medicine* 9, no. 11 (2013): 1195–1200.

15. Ahmad Afaghi, Helen O'Connor, and Chin Moi Chow, "High-Glycemic-Index Carbohydrate Meals Shorten Sleep Onset," *American Journal of Clinical Nutrition* 85, no. 2 (2007): 426–430.

16. S. H. A. Holt, H. J. Delargy, C. L. Lawton, and J. E. Blundell, "The Effects of High-Carbohydrate vs High-Fat Breakfasts on Feelings of Fullness and Alertness, and Subsequent Food Intake," *International Journal of Food Sciences and Nutrition* 50, no. 1 (1999): 13–28.

17. James P. Burton, Jenny M. Hoobler, and Melinda L. Scheuer, "Supervisor Workplace Stress and Abusive Supervision: The Buffering Effect of Exercise," *Journal of Business and Psychology* 27, no. 3 (2012): 271–279.

18. Amber J. Tietzel and Leon C. Lack, "The Short-Term Benefits of Brief and Long Naps Following Nocturnal Sleep Restriction," *Sleep* 24, no. 3 (2001): 293–300.

19. Sara C. Mednick, Denise J. Cai, Jennifer Kanady, and Sean P. A. Drummond, "Comparing the Benefits of Caffeine, Naps and Placebo on Verbal, Motor and Perceptual Memory," *Behavioural Brain Research* 193, no. 1 (2008): 79–86.

20. Tom M. McLellan, John A. Caldwell, and Harris R. Lieberman, "A Review of Caffeine's Effects on Cognitive, Physical and Occupational Performance," *Neuroscience and Biobehavioral Reviews* 71 (2016): 294–312.

21. Crystal F. Haskell, David O. Kennedy, Keith A. Wesnes, and Andrew B. Scholey, "Cognitive and Mood Improvements of Caffeine in Habitual Consumers and Habitual Non-consumers of Caffeine," *Psychopharmacology* 179, no. 4 (2005): 813–825.

22. Yu-Kai Chang, J. D. Labban, J. I. Gapin, and Jennifer L. Etnier, "The Effects of Acute Exercise on Cognitive Performance: A Meta-Analysis," *Brain Research* 1453 (2012): 87–101.

23. Charles H. Hillman, Kirk I. Erickson, and Arthur F. Kramer, "Be Smart, Exercise Your Heart: Exercise Effects on Brain and Cognition," *Nature Reviews Neuroscience* 9, no. 1 (2008): 58–65.

24. Chang et al., "The Effects of Acute Exercise on Cognitive Performance: A Meta-Analysis."

25. Ibid.

26. Ibid.

27. Ibid.

Step 8: Avoid Distractions

1. Robert E. Kaplan and Robert B. Kaiser, *Fear Your Strengths: What You Are Best at Could Be Your Biggest Problem* (San Francisco:

Berrett-Koehler Publishers, 2013); Silvia Moscoso and Jesús F. Salgado, "'Dark Side' Personality Styles as Predictors of Task, Contextual, and Job Performance," *International Journal of Selection and Assessment* 12, no. 4 (2004): 356–362.

2. D. L. Joseph, J. Jin, D. A. Newman, and E. H. O. Boyle, "Why Does Self-reported Emotional Intelligence Predict Job Performance? A Meta-Analytic Investigation of Mixed EI," *Journal of Applied Psychology* 100 (2015): 298–342.

3. Tomas Chamorro-Premuzic, "Emotional Intelligence Is Not Quite Total B.S.," *Talent Quarterly*, no. 14 (August 2017): 41–43.

4. Joseph et al., "Why Does Self-reported Emotional Intelligence Predict Job Performance?," 298.

5. D. L. Joseph and D. A. Newman, "Emotional Intelligence: An Integrative Meta-Analysis and Cascading Model," *Journal of Applied Psychology* 95, no. 1 (2010): 54.

6. Anders Ericsson and Robert Pool, "Malcolm Gladwell Got Us Wrong: Our Research Was Key to the 10,000-Hour Rule, But Here's What Got Oversimplified," *Salon*, April 10, 2016, http://www.salon.com/2016/04/10/malcolm_gladwell_got_us_wrong_our_research_was_key_to_the_10000_hour_rule_but_heres_what_got_oversimplified/.

7. David Z. Hambrick, Erik M. Altmann, Frederick L. Oswald, Elizabeth J. Meinz, Fernand Gobet, and Guillermo Campitelli, "Accounting for Expert Performance: The Devil Is in the Details," *Intelligence* 45 (2014): 112–114.

8. Angela Duckworth, *Grit: The Power of Passion and Perseverance* (New York: Simon and Schuster, 2016).

9. M. Credé, M. C. Tynan, and P. D. Harms, "Much Ado about Grit: A Meta-Analytic Synthesis of the Grit Literature," *Journal of Personality and Social Psychology* 113, no. 1 (2017).

10. Bill George, "The Truth About Authentic Leaders," Harvard Business School Working Knowledge, July 16, 2016, http://hbswk.hbs.edu/item/the-truth-about-authentic-leaders#comments.

11. Todd Schofield, "How to Adopt the Silicon Valley Mindset," Standard Chartered, Beyond Borders, https://www.sc.com/BeyondBorders/adopt-silicon-valley-mindset/.

12. Heidi Grant and Carol S. Dweck, "Clarifying Achievement Goals and Their Impact," *Journal of Personality and Social Psychology* 85, no. 3 (2003): 541.

13. Carol S. Dweck and Ellen L. Leggett, "A Social-Cognitive Approach to Motivation and Personality," *Psychological Review* 95, no. 2 (1988): 256.

14. Ian J. Deary et al., "The Stability of Individual Differences in Mental Ability from Childhood to Old Age: Follow-up of the 1932 Scottish Mental Survey," *Intelligence* 28, no. 1 (2000): 49–55.

15. Kira O. McCabe, Nico W. Van Yperen, Andrew J. Elliot, and Marc Verbraak, "Big Five Personality Profiles of Context-Specific Achievement Goals," *Journal of Research in Personality* 47, no. 6 (2013): 698–707.

16. Dana R. Carney, Amy J. C. Cuddy, and Andy J. Yap, "Power Posing: Brief Nonverbal Displays Affect Neuroendocrine Levels and Risk Tolerance," *Psychological Science* 21, no. 10 (2010): 1363–1368.

17. Maquita Peters, "'Power Poses' Co-Author: 'I Do Not Believe the Effects Are Real,'" National Public Radio, October 1, 2016, http://www.npr.org/2016/10/01/496093672/power-poses-co-author-i-do-not-believe-the-effects-are-real; Eva Ranehill et al., "Assessing the Robustness of Power Posing: No Effect on Hormones and Risk Tolerance in a Large Sample of Men and Women," *Psychological Science* 26, no. 5 (2015): 653–656.

Appendix

1. Samuel D. Gosling, Peter J. Rentfrow, and William B. Swann, "A Very Brief Measure of the Big-Five Personality Domains," *Journal of Research in Personality* 37, no. 6 (2003): 504–528.

INDEX

ABOUT THE AUTHOR

MARC EFFRON is the founder and president of the Talent Strategy Group, where he leads the firm's global consulting, education, executive search, and publishing businesses. His clients include the world's largest and most complex organizations in the for-profit, not-for-profit, and NGO sectors. Effron's signature approach to talent management, as espoused in his books and his consulting, is science-based simplicity.

He founded and publishes *Talent Quarterly* magazine and is the coauthor of the bestselling Harvard Business Review Press book *One Page Talent Management*. He also cofounded the Talent Management Institute at the University of North Carolina. Before forming the Talent Strategy Group, Marc served as vice president, talent management, for Avon Products and led the global leadership consulting practice for Aon Hewitt. He was also senior vice president, leadership development, for Bank of America and a congressional staff assistant. Marc is a sought-after speaker on talent management and leadership topics by both corporations and conferences.